VOLUME ONE

WHY *OUR* COMMUNITY NEEDS ARTIFICIAL INTELLIGENCE

FROM THE BEST SELLING AUTHOR

DASHAWN TAYLOR

BlaqGPT: Volume One

Why Our Community Needs Artificial Intelligence

www.BlaqGPT.com

For permissions requests, write to the publisher at:
Next Level Publishing
Email: info@nextlevelpublishing.com

First edition

DISCLAIMER
The information in this book is for educational purposes only. Due to the rapidly evolving nature of artificial intelligence, some content may become outdated. This book does not constitute professional, financial, legal, or career advice Readers should consult appropriate professionals for their specific circumstances. The author and publisher disclaim all warranties and shall not be liable for any damages resulting from use of this information.

Paperback Edition
ISBN: 979-8-9955894-8-8

Hardcover Edition
ISBN: 979-8-9955894-1-9

Editing by: Linda Day
Cover/Interior Design by Next Level Publishing

My uncle bought a thousand Blockbuster DVDs the same year Netflix started streaming. My aunt bought an encyclopedia set in 2005, the year Wikipedia became free. My cousin got really good at MySpace layouts in 2009,
two years after everyone moved to Facebook.
Some people have a pattern. They show up late, invest heavy, and get comfortable right before everything changes.
With AI, none of us can afford to be late again.

BlaqGPT
VOLUME ONE

TABLE OF CONTENTS

INTRODUCTION

I will never forget the look on his face.

It was the summer of 2000, and I was standing on a street corner in the heart of the city, handing out flyers for my new website. Not just any website. This was going to be the destination for hip hop culture online. News, music, videos, interviews, the whole nine. We'd poured everything into it. This was our shot at being part of the internet revolution everyone was talking about.

The flyer was simple: our logo, the URL (www.Real-Hiphop.com), and a tagline about bringing hip hop to the digital age. I handed one to a brother who looked exactly like our target audience. Fresh Timbs, fitted cap, clearly loved the culture. He took the flyer, looked at it, flipped it over like he was searching for something, then looked back up at me with the most confused expression I'd ever seen.

"So... what do I do with this?" he asked.

"You go to the website," I said, pointing at the URL. "Type that into your browser and you'll see everything. New music, interviews, all the latest."

He cut me off. "Man, I don't even have a computer. Maybe I can check this out when I get to the library or something."

Then he handed the flyer back to me and walked away. That moment has haunted me for over two decades. Not because he rejected what we built, but because of what that moment represented. Here we were, right at the dawn of the internet age, the biggest wealth creation opportunity in modern history, and our people were still trying to figure out where they could access a computer. While Silicon Valley was minting millionaires and billionaires, our community was asking for library cards.

We weren't just behind. We didn't even know we were in a race.

The Same Movie, Different Decade

That hip hop website we launched in 2000? We were pioneers, actually. One of the first to bring the authentic culture of hip hop to the internet in a real way. Not some corporate version, but the actual streets, the real voices, the culture we lived and breathed. We understood that hip hop wasn't just music. It was a movement, a lifestyle, a language. And we wanted to translate all of that energy and creativity into the digital space.

But we ran into the same wall over and over again. People loved hip hop. They watched *Yo! MTV Raps* religiously. They bought *The Source Magazine* and *XXL* every month. They listened to Hot 97 and Power 105 like it was the gospel.

They queued up for hours to get into concerts. They spent money on merchandise, CDs, and everything in between. The culture was thriving. But the internet? That was a different story.

"I don't really do the computer thing."

"That's too complicated for me."

"I'll wait until it's easier."

"Maybe when I have more time."

I heard every excuse, every hesitation, every reason why "right now" wasn't the right time. And I get it. Back then, getting online wasn't simple. You needed a computer, which was expensive. You needed an internet connection, which required a phone line and a monthly payment. You needed to understand how to navigate websites, which weren't as intuitive as they are now. There were real barriers.

But here's what kills me: while our community was waiting for things to get easier, other people were getting rich. Amazon started in 1994. By 2000, Jeff Bezos was already a billionaire. Google launched in 1998. By 2004, it made Larry Page and Sergey Brin two of the richest men alive. eBay, PayPal, Netflix. All these companies were born in the 90s and early 2000s.

And where were we? Handing back flyers because we didn't have computers.

The tech bubble burst in 2000, right around when we launched. Everyone said the internet was over, that it was all hype. But you know what? The internet wasn't over. It was just getting started. And the people who stayed in the game, who kept building and learning and adapting, they're the ones who own the world now.

We sat it out. Again.

History Keeps Repeating Itself

This isn't the first time this has happened to us. Not even close. Think about the Industrial Revolution. Black folks built the factories, laid the railroads, worked the machines. Our labor powered America's rise to becoming an economic superpower. But did we own the factories? Did we get stock in the railroad companies? Did we build generational wealth from the industries we literally built with our hands?

You already know the answer.

Then came the Computer Age in the 70s and 80s. Personal computers started showing up in homes and businesses. Tech companies started sprouting up in garages in California. Fortunes were made. Empires were built. And once again, we were largely on the outside looking in. Not because we weren't smart enough, not because we weren't capable, but because we weren't invited, weren't funded, weren't given access to the rooms where these decisions were being made.

By the time the Internet Age rolled around in the 90s and 2000s, we'd seen this movie twice already. But somehow, we still didn't recognize the pattern. We were still waiting at the library. Still saying "maybe later." Still convinced that this tech stuff wasn't for us.

And now? Now we're in the AI Revolution.

And I'm watching the exact same thing happen all over again.

Déjà Vu All Over Again

I see it everywhere I go. I talk to people in our community. Good people, smart people, hardworking people. And when I bring up artificial intelligence, I see that same look. That same deer in the headlights confusion from 2000.

"AI? Man, that's not for me. That's for tech people."

"I don't know anything about computers like that."

"That stuff is too complicated."

"I'll wait until it's more user-friendly."

I'm hearing the same excuses, the same hesitations, the same reasons to wait. And meanwhile, the world is moving at lightning speed.

ChatGPT launched in November 2022. Within five days, it had one million users. Within two months, it had one hundred million users. It's the fastest growing application in history. Companies are integrating AI into everything. Jobs are changing. Industries are being disrupted. Wealth is being created at a pace we've never seen before.

And we're saying "maybe later."

Do you know what kills me the most? It's not even that we're behind. It's that we don't seem to realize we CAN'T AFFORD to be behind this time.

Every previous technological revolution made the wealth gap wider. Every single one. The people who were early got rich. The people who were late got left behind. And the people who sat it out completely? They got erased.

This time, the stakes are even higher.

AI isn't just going to change some jobs. It's going to change ALL jobs. It's not just going to create new opportunities. It's going to eliminate old ones. It's not just going to shift the economy. It's going to redefine it completely. And if we sit this one out, we won't just be behind.

We'll be invisible.

Why I'm Writing This Book

I'm writing this book because I'm tired of watching this movie. I'm tired of seeing our community show up late to every revolution, every innovation, every opportunity.

I'm tired of hearing excuses about why "this isn't for us" when we've proven throughout history that there's nothing we can't master when we put our minds to it.

I'm tired of watching other communities build wealth, power, and influence using tools that are available to ALL of us, while we convince ourselves that we need permission, or special training, or some magic degree before we can even try. But most of all, I'm tired of the pattern.

Because here's the thing: I've lived this before. I watched it happen with the internet. I tried to warn people then. I tried to show them what was coming. And some people listened, but most didn't. And now, twenty five years later, I'm watching those same people, or their children, struggle because they missed that wave.

I don't want to watch it happen again. This book isn't just information. It's a intervention. It's a wake up call. It's me grabbing you by the shoulders and saying: We cannot afford to sit this one out.

This is not hype. This is not exaggeration. This is not me trying to sell you something. This is me telling you the truth because I love our people too much to watch us get left behind again.

This Time Can Be Different

Here's what gives me hope: AI is different from every other technological revolution we've seen.

When the internet started, you needed expensive equipment. You needed technical knowledge. You needed access to resources that many of us didn't have. The barriers to entry were real.

But AI? AI is accessible in ways previous technologies weren't. You can start learning AI today, for free, from your phone. You don't need a computer science degree. You don't need expensive software. You don't need venture capital or connections or permission from anyone.

The tools are here. The resources are available. The door is open. The only question is: Are we going to walk through it? Because make no mistake. This door won't stay open forever. Right now, we're in the early days. The people who get in now, who learn now, who build now, they're going to be the ones who shape what AI becomes. They're going to be the ones who own the companies, create the jobs, build the wealth, and wield the power.

Five years from now, it might be too late. The winners will be decided. The market will be captured. The opportunities will be gone. But right now? Right now we have a chance.

Who This Book Is For

This book is for you if you've ever felt like technology

is moving too fast and leaving you behind. This book is for you if you've heard about AI but don't really understand what it is or why it matters. This book is for you if you're tired of watching other people get rich while you struggle to keep up. This book is for you if you want better for your children but don't know how to give it to them.

This book is for you if you're scared that AI is going to take your job and you don't know what to do about it. This book is for you if you've ever been told, or told yourself, that "tech stuff" isn't for people like us. This book is for you if you're ready to stop being a consumer and start being a creator. This book is for you if you're tired of the same old pattern and ready to break the cycle.

But most importantly, this book is for you if you believe, even just a little bit, that we deserve more. That our community deserves to be part of the future, not just watching it happen to us. That our children deserve to inherit wealth and opportunity, not just struggle and survival. If that's you, then you're in the right place.

What This Book Will Do

I'm not going to lie to you: this book is going to make you uncomfortable. It has to. Because comfort is what got us here. Comfort is what made us wait. Comfort is what convinced us that we had time, that we could catch up later, that someone else would figure it out.

But I'm also going to give you hope. Because while the truth is uncomfortable, the opportunity is real.

In the pages ahead, I'm going to:

Show you the pattern. How we've been left behind before, why it happened, and how it's happening again right now with AI.

Explain what AI actually is. No jargon, no technical nonsense. Just plain English explanations that anyone can understand.

Reveal what's at stake. The jobs that are disappearing, the opportunities that are emerging, and why this matters for your future and your children's future.

Expose who's building AI. And why the fact that we're not in those rooms is a crisis that affects all of us. Break down the real cost of sitting this out. Not just in money, but in power, representation, and dignity.

Prove that you CAN do this. By destroying the excuses and showing you that this isn't as hard as you think.

Inspire you with stories of people like us who are already winning in AI. Because representation matters, and you need to see that this is possible.

And finally, **give you a clear path forward.** Because this book isn't just about the problem. It's about the solution.

What This Book Won't Do

This book is not going to teach you how to code. That's not what Volume One is about. This book is about why. Why you need to care about AI, why you need to get involved, why you can't afford to wait.

Volume Two will be the "how." The practical, step by step guide to actually learning and using AI. But you can't get to "how" until you understand "why." And if I do my job right, by the time you finish this book, you'll be hungry for Volume Two.

This book is also not going to sugarcoat things. I'm not going to pretend the challenges aren't real or that this is going to be easy. But I'm also not going to let you use those challenges as an excuse to do nothing.

A Promise and a Challenge

Here's my promise to you: If you read this book with an open mind and an honest heart, you will see AI differently. You will see our community's relationship with technology differently. You will see yourself differently.

And here's my challenge to you: Don't just read this book. **Act on it.** Reading is not enough. Understanding is not enough. Even agreeing with everything I say is not enough. The only thing that matters is what you DO with this information.

Because here's the truth: I can write this book, but I can't make you walk through the door. I can show you the opportunity, but I can't make you seize it. I can sound the alarm, but I can't make you wake up.

That part is on you.

The Choice

Twenty five years ago, I stood on a street corner trying to bring our people into the digital age. I watched opportunity slip through our fingers because we convinced ourselves we weren't ready.

Today, I'm writing this book to make sure that doesn't

happen again. The AI revolution is here. It's not coming. It's already arrived. And we have a choice to make. We can sit on the sidelines again, convincing ourselves that this isn't for us, that we'll catch up later, that someone else will figure it out. We can watch other communities build generational wealth while we struggle to keep up. We can let history repeat itself one more time.

Or we can do something different.

We can show up. We can learn. We can build.

We can compete.

We can win.

We can be early instead of late for once in our lives.

We can be creators instead of just consumers.

We can be the ones writing the future instead of reacting to it.

But it starts with a decision. Your decision. Right here, right now, on this page. Are you going to hand the flyer back and walk away? Or are you going to see what's possible?
The choice is yours. But I'm begging you: Please don't choose to sit this one out. Our ancestors survived slavery, Jim Crow, red lining, mass incarceration, and every other attempt to break us. They did that so we could have opportunities they never dreamed of.

This is one of those opportunities.

Don't waste it.

Let's get to work.

CHAPTER ONE

THE CYCLE KEEPS REPEATING

A friend of mine from college told me a story about his grandfather that stuck with me for years.

His grandfather worked on the railroads in the 1950s. Backbreaking work. Twelve hour days in the blazing sun, laying track across the country. He'd come home exhausted, hands calloused and bleeding, barely able to eat dinner before he collapsed into bed. He did this for years.

One day, my friend asked him why he did it. Why put his body through that kind of punishment?

His grandfather looked at him with tired eyes and said, "Because I thought if I worked hard enough, if I helped build something great, I'd be part of it. I thought my children would benefit from what I was building."

Then he paused and added something my friend never forgot: "Turned out I was just the hammer. And when the house was built, they put the hammer back in the shed."

When my friend told me this story, I didn't fully grasp the weight of it. But now, after researching the history, after talking to dozens of people in our community, after watching the internet revolution pass us by, I finally get it.

We keep being the hammer. And it's time we asked ourselves a hard question: How many times are we going to let this happen?

The Pattern We Can't Ignore

History has a way of repeating itself, especially when we refuse to learn from it. There's a pattern that's played out over and over again for the last two hundred years in America.

It goes like this:

Step One: A new industry or technology emerges that promises to change everything.

Step Two: That industry needs workers. Lots of them. Hard workers. People willing to do the difficult, dangerous, physically demanding labor that makes the whole thing possible.

Step Three: Black folks show up. We work. We build. We pour our blood, sweat, and tears into making this new thing successful.

Step Four: The industry matures. Wealth is created. Fortunes are made. Companies go public. Generational wealth is built.

Step Five: We look around and realize we own nothing. We built it, but we don't own it. We powered it, but we don't profit from it. We made it possible, but we're not invited to the table where the real decisions are made.

Step Six: The wealth gap gets wider. The opportunity gap gets deeper. And we're left wondering how it happened again.

This isn't conspiracy theory. This isn't paranoia. This is documented American history. And if we don't break this pattern with AI, we're going to be having the same conversation twenty years from now, watching our children and grandchildren wonder why they got left behind too. Let me show you what I mean.

The Industrial Revolution: We Built the Foundation

Let's start at the beginning. The Industrial Revolution in America, roughly from the 1860s through the early 1900s. This was the period when America transformed from an agricultural society into an industrial powerhouse. Factories, railroads, steel mills, textile plants. This is when America became an economic giant on the world stage.

And Black labor made it possible.

After the Civil War, millions of formerly enslaved people were technically free. But freedom without economic opportunity is just a different kind of prison. So Black folks went where the work was. The factories. The mills. The mines. The railroads.

We worked in the steel mills of Pittsburgh, breathing in toxic fumes, working fourteen hour shifts in temperatures that could literally cook a man alive. We worked in the coal mines of West Virginia and Kentucky, descending into darkness every day knowing there was a real chance we wouldn't come back up. We worked in the meatpacking plants of Chicago, doing the most dangerous jobs that white workers refused to do.

We laid the railroad tracks that connected the East Coast

to the West Coast. Do you know how the Transcontinental Railroad was built? Black workers and Chinese immigrants doing the impossible. Blasting through mountains. Laying track across deserts. Building bridges over canyons. Dying by the hundreds from accidents, disease, and exposure.

Stories like my friend's grandfather were common. Men who broke their bodies for railroad companies that would never put their names on anything.

We were there. We built it. Our labor made the Industrial Revolution possible.

And what did we get for it? Poverty wages. Company housing that we had to rent from the same people who employed us. Company stores where we had to buy goods at inflated prices. By the time you paid your rent and bought your food, you owed the company more than you made. It was slavery with a paycheck.

Meanwhile, the Rockefellers, the Carnegies, the Vanderbilts, they became the richest people in the world. Generational wealth that still exists today. Their great great grandchildren are still living off the fortunes built during the Industrial Revolution.

Where are the Black Rockefellers? Where are the Black Carnegies? They don't exist. Because we were the labor, not the owners. We were the hammer, not the carpenter.

The Railroad Boom: Connecting America on Our Backs

The railroads deserve their own section because they're the perfect example of how this pattern works. Between 1865 and 1900, America built over 160,000 miles of railroad track. That's enough track to circle the Earth six and a half times. It was the largest infrastructure project in human history up to that point.

The railroads changed everything. They connected the country. They enabled commerce on a scale never seen before. They made fortunes for the railroad barons. They created entire cities where the rails went through.

And Black workers built it.

After the Civil War, railroad companies actively recruited Black workers because they could pay us less than white workers and we had fewer options to refuse. We were cheaper. More desperate. Easier to exploit.

So we laid the track. We drove the spikes. We hauled the materials. We cleared the land. We built the bridges. We dug the tunnels.

It was brutal work. The injuries were constant. Arms crushed by equipment. Backs broken by falling materials. Men buried alive in cave ins. Heat stroke in the summer. Frostbite in the winter. And if you got hurt, you got fired. There was no workers' compensation. No safety regulations. No union to protect you.

The railroad companies didn't care. There was always another Black man desperate enough to take your place.

And when the work was done, when the last spike was driven and the railroads were complete, what did we get? A few weeks' wages. Maybe a handshake if we were lucky. And then we were dismissed.

The railroad barons became some of the wealthiest

men in America. Cornelius Vanderbilt died in 1877 with a fortune equivalent to over $200 billion in today's money. His wealth came from railroads that Black hands built.

But we didn't get stock options. We didn't get ownership stakes. We didn't get invited to join the boards of directors. We didn't build generational wealth. We just got tired. And old. And broken. And then we watched our children struggle because we had nothing to pass down to them except the advice to "work hard and maybe things will get better."

How'd that work out?

The Computer Age: Locked Out Before It Began

Fast forward to the 1970s and 1980s. The Computer Revolution is beginning. Personal computers are starting to show up in homes and businesses. Apple, Microsoft, IBM, they're all emerging. Silicon Valley is being born. Garages in California are turning into billion dollar companies.

This is it. This is the moment when everything changes. When knowledge work starts to replace manual labor. When you can build wealth with your mind instead of your body. When geography doesn't matter as much because you can connect with anyone, anywhere.

This should have been our moment. After generations of breaking our backs doing physical labor, here was an opportunity to compete on a more level playing field. You don't need to be big or strong to write code. You just need to be smart and willing to learn. But we weren't in the room.
Why not?

I've talked to so many people from that generation, and

the story is always the same. By the time personal computers came along, we were already multiple steps behind. The education gap. The wealth gap. The access gap. They all compounded.

In the 1980s, when home computers were becoming more common, they cost $2,000 to $3,000. That's the equivalent of about $6,000 to $9,000 today. A woman I met at a community event told me her parents couldn't even consider buying a computer. They were working two jobs each just to keep the lights on. Six grand on a machine that seemed like a toy? Impossible.

Even if you could afford a computer, you needed software. You needed books and training materials. You needed time to learn, which was hard when you were working multiple jobs just to make ends meet.

And even if you had the computer, the software, the books, and the time, you still needed to know that this was something you should be learning. You needed someone to tell you, "This computer thing isn't just a hobby. This is the future. This is where the money is going to be. This is what your kids need to know."

But nobody told us that.

Actually, that's not true. I've met Black educators and community leaders who saw what was coming and tried to sound the alarm. But they were voices in the wilderness, drowned out by more immediate concerns like crack cocaine devastating our neighborhoods, mass incarceration removing our men, and an economy that was leaving us further behind every year.

So while families in suburban neighborhoods were buying computers for their kids, teaching them to code, preparing them for the future, our kids were playing outside because we couldn't afford a computer. Or we had a computer but didn't know how to use it. Or we knew how to use it but didn't realize we should be teaching our kids to program.

And the gap got wider.

By the time the 1990s came around, the tech industry was booming. Startups were becoming billion dollar companies overnight. The dot com bubble was creating unprecedented wealth. Regular people were becoming millionaires because they happened to work at the right company at the right time.

But where were we?

Still barely represented in tech companies. Still underrepresented in computer science programs. Still locked out of the rooms where the decisions were being made and the equity was being distributed.

The statistics are brutal. In 1999, at the height of the dot com boom, Black people made up about 12% of the U.S. population but only 2.5% of computer science graduates. In Silicon Valley companies, the numbers were even worse. Less than 2% of employees at major tech companies were Black.

A mentor of mine who worked in tech during that era told me stories that made my blood boil. He was one of maybe three Black engineers at his company. When the company went public and everyone got rich from their stock options, he made good money. But he watched his white colleagues, who started at the same time with the same title, get promoted faster, get more stock, get invited into the inner circle where the real wealth was built. By the time the company was acquired, some of those colleagues were worth tens of millions. He was worth a fraction of that.

And it's not like we weren't capable. The few Black engineers and programmers who made it into the industry proved we could compete at the highest levels. But there were so few of us, and the barriers to entry were so high, that we never reached critical mass.

So when the wealth was distributed, we weren't in line to receive it. Stock options? Those went to the engineers and early employees, who were overwhelmingly white and Asian. Founder equity? That went to the entrepreneurs, who were overwhelmingly white and had access to venture capital and wealthy networks that we didn't.

Executive compensation? That went to the leadership teams, who looked nothing like our community. Even the secondary benefits passed us by. When tech workers got rich, they bought houses in certain neighborhoods, driving up property values. If you owned property in those neighborhoods, your wealth increased. But we didn't own property there. We were living in neighborhoods that were declining in value while tech neighborhoods were exploding. The Computer Age created trillions of dollars in wealth. And we got almost none of it. Again.

The Internet Boom: The Revolution We Watched Happen

Then came the Internet Revolution of the 1990s and

early 2000s, and this is where the stories I've heard become even more painful.

The internet should have been the great equalizer. For the first time in history, you didn't need a factory or a railroad or millions in capital to build something valuable. You needed a computer, an internet connection, and a good idea.

The barriers to entry were lower than they'd ever been. You could start a website for a few hundred dollars. You could reach millions of people without owning a printing press or a TV station. You could build a business from your bedroom. This was it. This was the opportunity we'd been waiting for.

And we missed it.

Amazon started in 1994. Jeff Bezos was selling books online from his garage. Today he's one of the richest people on Earth. A colleague told me about a Black entrepreneur he knew who had a similar idea around the same time. Wanted to sell books online. Went to banks for a loan. Got rejected over and over. "Nobody's going to buy books on the internet," they told him. Meanwhile, Bezos got funding and changed the world. That entrepreneur is still working a nine to five.

eBay launched in 1995. A platform where anyone could sell anything to anyone. The ultimate democratic marketplace. Today it's worth billions and has created thousands of millionaires. Were we selling on eBay in 1995? Some of us were, but not enough. Not nearly enough. I know people who were still having yard sales and selling out of car trunks in 2005, a full decade after eBay made it possible to reach millions of buyers from your living room.

Google was founded in 1998 by two Stanford students.

They built a search engine that became the gateway to the entire internet. Today they're worth over a trillion dollars. A professor I spoke with told me about brilliant Black computer science students during that era who had ideas just as innovative. But they couldn't get into Stanford or MIT. Couldn't get funding for their startups. Couldn't get meetings with venture capitalists. So their ideas died in dorm rooms while Google conquered the world.

PayPal launched in 1999. Digital payments. Revolutionized how money moves online. The founders and early employees became billionaires and went on to create Tesla, LinkedIn, YouTube, and dozens of other companies. How many Black folks were working at PayPal in 1999? I've asked around. The answer is always the same: almost none.

Facebook launched in 2004. Within a few years it had a billion users and made Mark Zuckerberg one of the richest people alive. The early employees got stock options worth millions. A high school friend told me he remembered when Facebook was just for college students. He was at an HBCU at the time. By the time Facebook opened up to his school, it was already huge. All the wealth had been distributed. He became a user, not an owner.

YouTube, Twitter, Instagram, Uber, Airbnb, all of them were founded in the 2000s and early 2010s. All of them created enormous wealth. All of them had the same pattern: founded by white or Asian entrepreneurs, funded by white or Asian venture capitalists, early employees who got rich were overwhelmingly white or Asian, and by the time we showed up, we were just users.

I've collected these stories from dozens of people. The entrepreneur who couldn't get a loan. The student who couldn't get into the right school. The engineer who couldn't get hired. The founder who couldn't get funded. All of them watching opportunities slip away while others got rich.

The Internet Revolution created more wealth faster than any previous technological revolution in human history. More millionaires and billionaires were minted in twenty years than in the previous two hundred years combined.
And our share? Less than 1%.

We were there. We used the internet. We shopped on Amazon. We searched on Google. We posted on Facebook. We watched YouTube videos. We took Ubers.

But we didn't own any of it. We didn't build any of it. We didn't profit from any of it. We were customers. Not creators. Not owners. Not beneficiaries. We were users in a system designed by others, built by others, and enriched by others. Once again, we were the hammer. And when the house was built, they put us back in the shed.

The Mobile Revolution: In Our Hands But Not Our Pockets

Just when you thought the pattern couldn't repeat itself again, along came smartphones. The iPhone launched in 2007. The App Store opened in 2008. Suddenly, anyone could build an app and distribute it to millions of people. The barriers to entry were incredibly low. You didn't need a storefront. You didn't need inventory. You didn't need a distribution network. You just needed a good app idea and some coding skills.

Apps started making people rich. Angry Birds, Instagram, WhatsApp, Snapchat, Flappy Bird, even simple utility apps were generating millions in revenue. And who was building these apps? Mostly the same demographics that had won in previous revolutions. Young white and Asian developers who had been coding since they were kids because their parents bought them computers in the 1990s.

Where were we?

I've seen the research. We were the most enthusiastic adopters of smartphones in America. Studies showed Black Americans were more likely to own smartphones and spent more time on them than any other demographic group.

We were power users. Early adopters. We made apps go viral. When Black Twitter decided something was trending, it trended. When we embraced an app, everyone else followed. But we weren't building the apps. We weren't the developers creating the next Instagram or Snapchat. We weren't the entrepreneurs raising venture capital to scale our app ideas.

Someone I mentor told me about his cousin who had an idea for a social app back in 2010. The idea was solid. Could have been the next big thing. But he didn't know how to code. Didn't know any developers. Didn't know how to raise money. Didn't have a network of people who could help him. So he watched other apps with similar ideas get built, get funded, and make their founders rich. His idea stayed an idea.

We were, once again, the consumers. The users. The cultural trendsetters who made other people's products valuable, but didn't capture any of that value for ourselves.

There were exceptions, of course. I've met Black developers and entrepreneurs who broke through. But they were so few, and the challenges they faced were so significant, that they proved the rule rather than breaking it.

The Mobile Revolution was literally in our hands. We had the devices. We had the passion. We had the creativity and cultural influence to make or break any app. But we didn't have the coding skills, the business knowledge, the access to capital, or the networks to turn our ideas into the next billion dollar company.

So we watched. Again. As another wave of wealth creation passed us by.

The Pattern Is Clear

Do you see it now?

Every major technological revolution for the last 150 years has followed the same pattern:

New technology emerges. It promises to change everything, create opportunities, democratize access to wealth. We show up. Sometimes as labor. Sometimes as users. Sometimes as enthusiastic early adopters.

Wealth is created. Enormous amounts of it. Generational wealth. World changing wealth. We're excluded from the wealth distribution. We're not the owners. We're not the founders. We're not the early employees with stock options. We're not the investors who get 100x returns. We're the workers who get wages, or the consumers who get products, but never the ownership.

The wealth gap grows. With each revolution, the

people who were already winning pull further ahead. And we fall further behind.

We tell ourselves it's okay. We convince ourselves that we're not tech people, or it's too complicated, or the barriers are too high. We make excuses. We wait for the next opportunity. We hope things will be different. The cycle repeats. A new technology comes along. And we do the same thing all over again.

This isn't about individual failure. This is about a systemic pattern that has played out over and over again. And right now, at this very moment, we're at the beginning of the next cycle.

The AI Revolution: Here We Go Again

Artificial Intelligence is the next revolution. It's not coming. It's here. And if you look closely, you can already see the pattern starting to play out. AI companies are being founded. AI research is being done. Mostly at universities and companies that have very few Black researchers. Venture capital is being invested. Billions of dollars flowing into AI startups. And less than 1% of it is going to Black founders.

Jobs are being created. High paying jobs for AI engineers, data scientists, machine learning specialists. Jobs that require skills most of us don't have because we weren't encouraged to pursue computer science degrees.

Products are being built. AI tools that will change how we work, live, communicate, and make decisions. And we're not building them. Other people are building them for us, which means they're building them with their values, their biases, their understanding of the world.

Wealth is being created. Right now. As you read this. AI companies are raising hundreds of millions of dollars. AI stocks are soaring. AI entrepreneurs are becoming billionaires. And where are we? I talk to people in our community every week. The responses are painfully familiar:

"AI? That's not for me. That's for tech people."

"I don't know anything about computers like that."

"That stuff is too complicated."

"I'll wait until it's more user friendly."

"Maybe my kids will get into that."

Do you hear it? It's the same script from every previous revolution. The same excuses. The same reasons to wait. The same belief that this isn't for us. And meanwhile, the train is leaving the station.

The Numbers Don't Lie

Let me show you some statistics that should terrify you. In 2023, venture capital firms invested over $25 billion in AI startups in the United States. Black founders received less than 1% of that money. Less than 1%. At the major AI companies like OpenAI, Google DeepMind, Anthropic, and Meta AI, Black researchers and engineers make up less than 3% of the workforce. Less than 3%. In AI research published at top conferences, less than 2% of papers have Black lead authors. Less than 2%.

In university computer science and AI programs, Black students make up less than 5% of graduate students.

Do you see where this is going?

By the time AI fully transforms the economy in five or ten years, the ownership will be decided. The wealth will be distributed. The opportunities will be captured.

And if we're only 1% to 3% of the people building AI, what do you think our share of the wealth will be? I'll tell you exactly what it'll be: the same percentage we got from every other technological revolution. Almost nothing.

Why This Time Is Different and Worse

Here's the part that keeps me up at night. Every previous technological revolution replaced some jobs and created new ones. The Industrial Revolution replaced farmers with factory workers. The Computer Revolution replaced typewriters with word processors. The Internet Revolution replaced retail stores with e commerce.

But people adapted. It took time, it was painful, but eventually new jobs emerged and people figured out how to make a living in the new economy. AI is different. AI isn't just replacing specific jobs. It's replacing entire categories of human capabilities. Writing. Analysis. Creative work. Decision making. Even coding itself. An AI can write an article in seconds. Design a logo in minutes. Analyze a legal document in moments. Generate a business plan faster than you can read this sentence.

And it's getting better every single day.

The jobs that are being eliminated aren't just factory jobs or data entry jobs. They're knowledge jobs. The jobs we were told to go to college for. The jobs that were supposed to be safe from automation.

Customer service? AI can handle it. Bookkeeping? AI can do it faster and cheaper. Graphic design? AI can generate thousands of options in seconds. Writing and content creation? AI can produce it at scale. Basic legal work? AI can review contracts and do research. Entry level coding? AI can write code now.

I'm not saying humans will be completely replaced in all these fields. But I am saying that one person with AI can do the work that used to take ten people. Which means nine of those people lose their jobs.

And who do you think will be first to go?

The people with the least power. The least connections. The least resources to adapt.

Us.

The Question We Have to Answer

So here's the question we have to ask ourselves:

Are we going to let this happen again?

Are we going to sit on the sidelines while another revolution creates trillions in wealth and we get none of it?

Are we going to watch our jobs get automated while other people use AI to build businesses and get rich?

Are we going to be consumers of AI technology built by others, with their biases and blind spots, that doesn't understand us or serve us?

Are we going to let our children grow up unprepared for an AI dominated world because we were too scared or too proud to learn something new?

Are we going to be the hammer one more time?

Or are we finally going to say: enough. Enough watching from the sidelines. Enough making excuses. Enough waiting for someone else to save us. Enough accepting scraps when we should be at the table. This is our moment. Right now. Today.

The AI revolution is in its early stages. The winners haven't been decided yet. The wealth hasn't all been distributed yet. The opportunities are still available. But the window is closing. Five years from now might be too late. The companies will be established. The talent will be hired. The market share will be captured. The wealth will be consolidated. We've been late to every revolution for 150 years. We cannot afford to be late to this one. The cycle has to end. The pattern has to break. And it starts with you making a decision right here, right now, that you're not going to let history repeat itself.

You're not going to be the hammer. You're going to be the carpenter. You're going to learn AI. You're going to understand AI. You're going to use AI. And if you're ambitious enough, you're going to build with AI. Because the alternative is unacceptable. The alternative is watching our children ask us twenty years from now: "Why didn't you do something when you had the chance?"

I don't know about you, but I refuse to have that conversation.

This ends now.

CHAPTER TWO

WHAT EXACTLY IS AI? (IN PLAIN ENGLISH)

Let me start with a confession: the tech industry has done an absolutely terrible job of explaining what AI actually is.

They've wrapped it in layers of jargon, technical terms, and mathematical concepts that make it sound like you need three PhDs just to have a conversation about it. They talk about "neural networks" and "machine learning algorithms" and "deep learning architectures" like everyone should just automatically know what that means.

And when regular people hear all that technical talk, what happens? They tune out. They decide it's not for them. They convince themselves that AI is something only engineers and computer scientists can understand.

That's exactly what I saw happen with a woman I met at a community workshop last year. She was in her late forties, worked in healthcare administration, smart as hell. When I mentioned I was writing a book about AI, she literally waved her hand and said, "Oh, that's too complicated for me. I'm not a computer person."

But here's what's wild: this same woman had been using AI all day, every day, for years. She just didn't know it.

She used her phone's voice assistant to set reminders and send texts while driving. She relied on her GPS to navigate the city. She let Netflix recommend shows for her and her kids. She used facial recognition to unlock her phone. She had a smart thermostat that learned her schedule and adjusted the temperature automatically.

She was surrounded by AI. Using it constantly. Benefiting from it daily.

She just didn't recognize it because nobody had ever explained to her, in plain English, what AI actually was.

That's what this chapter is about. We're going to strip away all the complicated language, all the technical jargon, all the intimidating terminology, and talk about AI the way regular people talk. No PhD required. No engineering degree necessary. Just straight talk about what this technology actually is and what it actually does.

Because here's the truth: AI isn't that complicated. The people who build it have made it seem complicated, but the basic concept? You can understand it. Your grandmother can understand it. Your kids definitely understand it because they've grown up with it.

So let's break it down.

What AI Actually Is

At its most basic level, artificial intelligence is just a computer program that can learn from experience and make decisions based on what it's learned.

That's it. That's the simple version.

Now, let me explain what I mean by "learn from experience" because that's the part that makes AI different from regular computer programs.

A traditional computer program is like a recipe. Someone writes out exact instructions, step by step, and the computer follows those instructions exactly. If this happens, do that. If that happens, do this other thing. Every possible situation is spelled out in advance by a human programmer.

But AI works differently. Instead of being programmed with specific instructions for every possible situation, AI is designed to figure things out on its own by looking at examples.

Think of it like teaching a child to recognize dogs. You don't give them a detailed technical description: "A dog is a four-legged mammal with fur, a tail, and a wet nose that barks." Instead, you just point at dogs and say, "That's a dog. That's a dog. That's also a dog." After seeing enough examples, the child figures out what makes something a dog, even if they've never seen that particular breed before.

That's essentially how AI works. You show it thousands or millions of examples, and it starts to recognize patterns. It learns what features matter and what features don't. And then, when it sees something new, it can make an educated guess based on all the examples it's seen before.

A guy I know who teaches middle school told me he explains it to his students like this: "AI is like a really good guesser that gets better at guessing the more practice it gets."

That's actually perfect. Because that's exactly what it is. When your phone's facial recognition unlocks when it sees your face, it's making a really educated guess that the face it's looking at is yours, based on thousands of times it's seen your face before.

When Netflix recommends a show, it's making a really educated guess that you'll like it, based on patterns it's noticed about what you've watched before and what people with similar tastes have enjoyed.

When your GPS reroutes you around traffic, it's making a really educated guess about which route will be fastest, based on patterns it's learned about traffic flow at different times of day.

It's all pattern recognition. That's the heart of AI.

Now, the tech industry uses fancy terms for this. They call it "machine learning" or "neural networks" or "deep learning." And yes, there are technical differences between these terms that matter to engineers. But for understanding what AI actually does? You just need to know it's a computer program that learns from examples and makes predictions based on patterns.

That's it. You just understood AI.

You're Already Using It Every Single Day

Here's what frustrates me: people think AI is this futuristic thing that's coming someday. Like it's something from a sci-fi movie that doesn't exist yet in real life.

But AI has been part of your daily routine for years. You've just been using it without thinking about it as "AI."

A cousin of mine realized this during a family dinner last Thanksgiving. Someone brought up AI and how scary it was, and she said, "Thank God I don't have to deal with any of that." I asked her how she got to dinner. "GPS," she said. How did she find the recipe she brought? "Googled it." What show was she binge-watching? "Oh, Netflix recommended it and it was so good."

The whole table got quiet as it sank in. She'd used AI at least a dozen times that day without even thinking about it. Let me walk you through a typical morning and show you how much AI you're probably already using.

You wake up to your phone alarm. If you use an iPhone or Android, your phone has been using AI all night. It learned your sleep patterns. It knows what time you usually go to bed and wake up. It adjusts its charging to preserve battery life based on when you typically unplug it. That's AI.

You check your email. The spam filter that keeps junk out of your inbox? AI. It learned what spam looks like by analyzing millions of emails. Your email app also uses AI to prioritize which messages show up at the top of your inbox, predicting which ones you're most likely to want to see first. You scroll through social media. Every post you see has been chosen by AI. Facebook, Instagram, Twitter, TikTok, they all use AI to decide what to show you and in what order. The algorithm learned what kind of content keeps you engaged based on what you've liked, commented on, and watched before.

You ask your voice assistant to play music or check the weather. That's AI processing your voice, understanding what you said, and responding appropriately. Ten years ago, voice recognition was terrible. Now it's so good we take it for granted. That improvement? AI.

You get in your car and use GPS to avoid traffic. The app is using AI to predict traffic patterns based on data from millions of other drivers, historical traffic data, current conditions, and even things like weather and time of day. You stop for coffee and the app remembers your usual order. AI learned your preferences.

You get to work and your computer suggests finishing your sentences as you type. AI predicting what you're trying to say.

You take a photo and your phone automatically adjusts the lighting, identifies faces, and even suggests filters. All AI. By lunchtime, you've probably interacted with AI dozens of times. And that's just the obvious stuff. Behind the scenes, AI is powering your credit card fraud detection, your bank's security systems, the autocorrect on your phone, and countless other things you never think about.

I had a conversation with a woman at a barbershop last month who insisted she'd never used AI. But she was holding a smartphone. She used Uber to get there. She'd been complaining about Netflix not having anything good to watch. When I pointed all this out, she laughed and said, "Wait, that's all AI? I thought AI was like robots and stuff."

And that's the disconnect. People have this image in their heads of AI as humanoid robots or super-intelligent computers that can think like humans. But the AI that actually exists and that you use every day is much more practical and much less dramatic.

It's not C-3PO from Star Wars. It's the thing that keeps your favorite shows queued up and your photos organized and your route optimized.

The Tools You Use Without Thinking About Them

Let me break down some of the most common AI tools you're probably using right now, just so you can start recognizing them.

Your Phone's Assistant. Whether it's Siri, Google Assistant, or Alexa, these are all AI-powered. They use something called natural language processing, which is just a fancy way of saying they can understand human speech. They learned by listening to millions of voice samples from people all over the world, figuring out patterns in how people talk, what words sound like, what questions people ask, and what answers make sense.

A friend's grandmother was amazed when I showed her that she could just talk to her phone and it would set timers, send texts, and answer questions. She'd been intimidated by technology her whole life, but voice assistants made sense to her because talking is natural. That's the power of well-designed AI. It meets you where you are.

Netflix, Spotify, and YouTube Recommendations.

These platforms use AI to study what you watch or listen to, then predict what else you might like. They look at patterns like: if you watched this show, you're likely to enjoy these other shows. If you listened to this song, here are similar songs. The more you use them, the better they get at predicting your tastes.

Now, sometimes they get it wrong. Sometimes Netflix recommends something you have zero interest in. That's because AI isn't perfect. It's making educated guesses, and sometimes the guess is wrong. But it's right often enough that you probably end up watching whatever it suggests more than you'd like to admit.

GPS and Maps. Google Maps, Waze, Apple Maps, they all use AI to predict traffic, suggest routes, and estimate arrival times. They're analyzing data from millions of users in real-time, learning patterns about how traffic flows, where accidents are likely to happen, when certain routes get congested, and which alternate routes are better at different times of day.

Someone told me they didn't trust GPS at first because it seemed too smart. "How does it know there's traffic before I get there?" It knows because it's constantly learning from everyone else who's driving. That's the power of AI at scale.

Facial Recognition. When your phone unlocks by looking at your face, that's AI. It created a mathematical model of your face the first time you set it up, and now it compares every face it sees to that model. If there's a match, it unlocks. Apple claims their facial recognition is sophisticated enough to work even if you grow a beard, change your hairstyle, or wear glasses.

Here's something interesting: facial recognition AI has historically been worse at recognizing Black faces than white faces. Why? Because the people training the AI didn't include enough Black faces in the training data. This is a perfect example of why representation matters in AI development. If the people building the technology don't look like us, they might not even think to test whether it works for us.

Autocorrect and Predictive Text. Every time your phone fixes a typo or suggests the next word you're trying to type, that's AI. It learned language patterns by analyzing billions of text messages, emails, and other written content. It knows that if you type "I'm on my," you're probably going to type "way" next. If you type "Good," at the beginning of a message in the morning, you're probably typing "Good morning."

An older man at a community center told me he hated autocorrect because it was always wrong. But when we looked at his phone, it was actually right about 80% of the time. He just remembered the times it failed. That's human nature. We notice the failures more than the successes. But AI doesn't have to be perfect to be useful.

Social Media Feeds. Instagram, Facebook, TikTok, Twitter, they all use AI to decide what posts show up in your feed and in what order. The algorithm learns what kind of content you engage with, then shows you more of that content. Like a lot of dog videos? You're going to see more dogs. Watch a lot of cooking content? Here come the recipes. This is where AI gets controversial, because these algorithms can create echo chambers where you only see content that reinforces what you already believe. But that's not really an AI problem. That's a design choice by the companies. The AI is just doing what it was told to do: keep you engaged. The consequences of that design choice? That's on the humans who made it.

What AI Can Actually Do

Now that we've established what AI is and where you're already using it, let's talk about what it's actually capable of. This is important because there's so much hype and misinformation out there. People either think AI can do everything or they think it's all smoke and mirrors. The truth is somewhere in the middle.

AI is exceptional at pattern recognition. This is its superpower. If you need to find patterns in huge amounts of data, AI is probably better at it than humans. This is why AI is so good at things like detecting credit card fraud, diagnosing certain diseases from medical images, predicting equipment failures in factories, and recommending products you might want to buy.

AI is great at repetitive tasks that require consistency. If you need something done the same way a million times, AI won't get tired or bored. It won't have an off day. It'll do the task exactly the same way every single time. This is why companies use AI for things like sorting emails, processing transactions, analyzing data, and quality control.

AI excels at processing huge amounts of information quickly. A human might be able to read a few hundred documents in a day. AI can process millions of documents in seconds. This makes it valuable for research, legal discovery, market analysis, and any other field where you need to sort through massive amounts of information.

AI is increasingly good at creative tasks. This one

surprises people. We used to think creativity was uniquely human. But AI can now write articles, compose music, create art, design logos, and even write code. It's doing this by learning patterns from millions of examples of human-created content and then generating new content based on those patterns.

A designer I know was initially threatened by AI art generators. But then she realized she could use them as a tool for brainstorming and rough drafts, then add her own creative vision to finish the work. The AI didn't replace her. It made her faster and more productive.

AI can have conversations that feel surprisingly human. Chatbots powered by AI can answer questions, provide customer service, offer recommendations, and even provide emotional support. They're not actually conscious or self-aware, but they're good enough at mimicking human conversation that it can be hard to tell you're talking to a machine.

AI can translate languages in real-time. The translation isn't always perfect, but it's good enough that you can have a conversation with someone who doesn't speak your language using your phone as a translator. That's pretty amazing.

These are real capabilities that exist right now. Not sci-fi stuff. Not future predictions. Things you can do with AI today.

What AI Cannot Do

But let's talk about the limits, because this is where a lot of the hype comes in.

AI cannot truly understand. This is the biggest

misconception. When AI answers a question or writes an essay or creates a piece of art, it doesn't actually understand what it's doing the way a human does. It's matching patterns. It's doing really sophisticated statistics. But there's no comprehension, no consciousness, no genuine understanding happening.

Think of it this way: you could train an AI to translate between English and Chinese by showing it millions of examples. It might get really good at translation. But it doesn't "know" either language the way a human bilingual person does. It's just learned the patterns of how words and phrases correspond.

AI cannot feel or have genuine emotions. When a chatbot says "I understand how you feel," it doesn't actually understand. It's generating a response that it's learned is appropriate in that context based on patterns in its training data. There's no empathy, no actual feeling, no real emotional connection.

AI cannot truly innovate or be creative in the human sense. AI can generate new combinations of things it's seen before. It can remix and recombine in surprising ways. But it can't have an original insight or a creative breakthrough that comes from nowhere. Everything it creates is derivative of what it was trained on.

A musician told me he's not worried about AI replacing human artists because AI can only create variations of what already exists. True innovation, true creativity, comes from human experience, emotion, culture, and perspective. AI doesn't have any of that.

AI cannot explain its reasoning in most cases. This is a big problem. When AI makes a decision, it often can't tell you why. It processed millions of data points, found patterns, and came to a conclusion. But it can't break down its reasoning in a way humans can understand. This is called the "black box" problem, and it's a real issue when AI is making important decisions about things like loan approvals or medical diagnoses.

AI cannot work without training data. AI needs examples to learn from. Lots of them. If you want AI to do something completely new that has no training data, it can't do it. A human expert might be able to figure it out through reasoning and creativity. AI needs to see examples first.

AI cannot detect its own biases or errors. If the training data is biased, the AI will be biased. If there are errors in the training data, the AI will learn those errors. It has no way to step back and say, "Wait, this doesn't make sense" or "This seems unfair." That requires human oversight.

AI cannot operate outside its training. If you train an AI to identify cats and dogs, then show it a picture of a horse, it's going to guess either cat or dog because those are the only categories it knows. It can't spontaneously create a new category called "horse" without being trained on horses.

AI cannot set its own goals or values. This is crucial to understand. AI doesn't want anything. It doesn't have desires or motivations. It does exactly what it was programmed to do, nothing more, nothing less. All those sci-fi movies about AI taking over the world and deciding humans are obsolete? That's not how AI works. AI has no agency, no will, no goals beyond what humans give it.

A woman at a book club I visited was terrified of AI

because she'd seen too many movies about robots becoming evil. I had to explain that the AI we have now is nothing like that. It's a tool. A very powerful tool, but just a tool. It's like being afraid your calculator will decide to take over the world. It doesn't work that way.

Why It Seems More Complicated Than It Is

So if AI is really just pattern recognition and prediction, why does it seem so complicated and intimidating?
Several reasons.

First, the tech industry benefits from making it seem complicated. If AI seems like magic that only specially trained experts can understand, then those experts become more valuable. There's money and power in being the gatekeeper to understanding. So there's not a lot of incentive for tech companies to explain things in simple terms.

Second, the math behind AI is genuinely complex. Even though the concept is simple (learn from examples, find patterns, make predictions), the actual mathematical techniques used to do that are sophisticated. But here's the thing: you don't need to understand the math to understand what AI does and how to use it. Just like you don't need to understand how an engine works to drive a car.

Third, AI touches multiple technical fields. Computer science, statistics, mathematics, cognitive science, neuroscience, they all play a role in AI development. So when experts talk about AI, they're drawing on jargon from multiple disciplines, which makes it even harder for outsiders to follow.

Fourth, the media loves to hype AI. Every article about AI makes it sound either like the most amazing thing ever created or like the apocalypse is coming. The truth is much more boring: AI is a useful tool with both benefits and limitations. But "AI is pretty useful for some things and not others" doesn't make for a clickable headline.

Fifth, there's a lot of marketing spin. Companies slap "AI-powered" on everything now because it sounds cutting-edge, even when the AI component is minimal or not even real AI. This creates confusion about what AI actually is and what it can do.

But once you understand the basic concept (pattern recognition through learning from examples), most of the mystery disappears. You can watch AI announcements and read articles about AI developments and actually understand what's being talked about.

You Don't Need A PhD To Get This

I want to emphasize this point because it's crucial: you do not need to be a technical expert to understand AI, use AI, or even work with AI.

Yes, building AI systems from scratch requires serious technical expertise. But using AI? That's being designed to be as simple as possible. The companies creating AI tools want as many people as possible to use them. So they're making the interfaces simple and intuitive.

A teacher I know was convinced she couldn't use any AI tools because she "wasn't techy enough." Then I showed her ChatGPT. You type a question or request in plain English, it gives you an answer. That's it. She was using it within five minutes to help create lesson plans and generate quiz questions. No technical knowledge required.

The same goes for AI image generators, AI writing assistants, AI coding tools, and dozens of other applications. They're designed for regular people to use.

Think about it this way: do you need to understand how streaming works to watch Netflix? Do you need to know how GPS satellites communicate to use Google Maps? Do you need to understand algorithmic recommendations to use Spotify?

Of course not. You just use the tools.

AI is the same way. The barrier to using AI is much lower than most people think.

Now, there is a difference between using AI tools and understanding AI well enough to make informed decisions about AI policy, AI ethics, and AI's impact on society. That requires more knowledge. But even that doesn't require a PhD. It just requires curiosity and a willingness to learn.

A grandmother in her seventies told me she made a point of learning about AI because she wanted to understand what her grandkids were growing up with. She watched YouTube tutorials, read articles written for general audiences, and played around with some AI tools. She's not an expert, but she understands enough to have informed opinions and conversations. If she can do it, anyone can.

The Real Question Isn't "Can I Understand AI?"

The real question is: "Am I willing to learn?"

Because here's what I've discovered talking to hundreds of people in our community: the ones who say they can't understand AI haven't actually tried. They've looked at some jargon-filled technical article or listened to some expert speaking in code, decided it was too hard, and given up before they even started.

But the ones who approach it with curiosity, who ask questions, who play around with some AI tools, who watch some beginner-friendly tutorials, they get it. Maybe not every technical detail, but enough to use AI effectively and understand its implications.

The barrier isn't intelligence. It's not education level. It's not age. It's not technical background.

The barrier is believing you can't do it.

And I'm here to tell you: you absolutely can.

In the next chapters, we're going to talk about how AI is already changing the job market, who's building these systems, and what we stand to lose if we sit this revolution out. But none of that will mean anything if you're still convinced that AI is too complicated for you to understand.

It's not.

You just understood it. You know what AI is now. You recognize it in your daily life. You understand what it can and can't do. You know why it seems more complicated than it really is.

That's the foundation. That's all you need to move forward. Now let's talk about what's at stake.

CHAPTER THREE

THE DIFFERENT FLAVORS OF AI

Now that you understand what AI is at its core, we need to talk about the different types of AI you're going to encounter. Because here's the thing: when people say "AI," they're usually talking about very different technologies that happen to share the same label.

It's like saying "vehicle." A bicycle is a vehicle. A Honda Civic is a vehicle. An eighteen wheeler truck is a vehicle. A fighter jet is a vehicle. Technically they're all the same category, but they work completely differently and serve completely different purposes.

AI is the same way. The AI that writes emails for you is completely different from the AI that drives a Tesla. The AI that recommends movies on Netflix is completely different from the AI that reads X-rays in hospitals. They're all "AI," but they're built differently, trained differently, and used for different things.

Why does this matter?

Because each type of AI represents different

opportunities. Different career paths. Different business possibilities. Different ways you could use AI to improve your life or serve your community.

If you only understand AI as one monolithic thing, you might miss the opportunities that are right in front of you. But if you understand the different types, you can identify which ones are relevant to your life, your work, your interests, and your goals.

A woman I spoke with last year worked in customer service for a healthcare company. She was worried that AI was going to take her job. And she was right to worry, because chatbots are getting really good at handling routine customer service questions. But when we talked about the different types of AI, she realized that voice AI and language models could actually make her better at her job. She could use AI to help draft responses, translate for non-English speakers, and handle the repetitive parts of her work so she could focus on the complex cases that actually needed a human touch.

She didn't get replaced by AI. She learned to work with AI and became more valuable because of it.

That's what understanding the different types of AI can do for you. So let's break them down.

Language Models: AI That Reads and Writes

This is probably the type of AI that's gotten the most attention recently, and for good reason. Language models like ChatGPT, Claude, and others have changed the game in terms of what AI can do with written and spoken language.

Here's what language models actually are: AI systems

that have been trained on massive amounts of text from the internet, books, articles, and other sources. They learned patterns in how language works. How sentences are structured. How conversations flow. How different topics are typically discussed. And now they can generate human-like text in response to prompts.

Think of it like this: if you've read thousands of novels, you start to develop an intuition for how stories work. You can predict what might happen next. You understand the rhythm of dialogue. You know what feels right and what feels off. Language models have done something similar, except instead of reading thousands of books, they've analyzed billions of pieces of text.

What can language models do?

Writing assistance. They can help you write emails, reports, articles, social media posts, or pretty much anything that involves written language. You give them a topic or a prompt, and they can generate text. The quality varies, and it always needs human review and editing, but it can speed up the writing process dramatically.

I know a pastor who uses ChatGPT to help brainstorm sermon outlines. He still writes the sermons himself, adds his own stories and perspectives, and delivers them in his own voice. But the AI helps him organize his thoughts and consider different angles he might not have thought of. He's not replacing his spiritual work with AI. He's using AI as a tool to enhance his ministry.

Conversation and customer service. Language models power chatbots that can have natural-sounding conversations with customers, answer questions, provide information, and even handle complaints. They're not perfect, and they can't handle everything a human customer service rep can, but they can handle the routine stuff, which frees up human workers to deal with complex issues.

Translation. While translation AI has existed for a while, language models have made it significantly better. They can translate between languages while preserving tone, context, and nuance much better than older translation systems.

Summarization. They can read long documents and create concise summaries. This is valuable for anyone who needs to process a lot of information quickly.

Code generation. Surprisingly, language models can write computer code. You describe what you want a program to do in plain English, and they can generate the code. It's not always perfect, but it's gotten good enough that even professional programmers use it to speed up their work.

A nephew of mine is learning to code using ChatGPT. When he gets stuck, he asks the AI to explain concepts or help debug his code. It's like having a patient tutor available 24/7. He's learning faster than he would have otherwise because he can get immediate help whenever he needs it.

Educational support. Language models can answer questions, explain concepts, provide examples, and even create practice problems. They're being used as tutoring tools, study aids, and teaching assistants.

Creative brainstorming. They can help generate ideas for projects, stories, businesses, or pretty much anything.

Again, the ideas need human filtering and refinement, but they can help get past creative blocks.

Here's what's important to understand about language models: they're tools for working with language in all its forms. And since so much of what we do involves language (writing, reading, communicating, teaching, learning), these tools have implications for almost every field.

The opportunity here? If your work involves writing, communicating, teaching, or processing information, learning to use language models effectively could make you significantly more productive. And if you're creative, you could build businesses or services that use these tools to solve problems in your community.

Image Generators: AI That Creates Visual Content

A year ago, AI-generated images were kind of a joke. You could tell they were AI-made because they looked weird and distorted. Hands had the wrong number of fingers. Faces looked slightly off. The images were interesting but not really usable for professional work.

Now? AI can generate images that are nearly indistinguishable from photographs or professional illustrations. And it's only getting better.

Image generators like DALL-E, Midjourney, Stable Diffusion, and others work similarly to language models, except instead of being trained on text, they were trained on millions of images and the text descriptions that go with those images. They learned patterns in how visual elements work together, what makes an image look realistic or artistic, and how to translate text descriptions into visual representations.

You type a description of what you want to see, and the AI generates an image based on that description. Want a picture of a futuristic city at sunset with flying cars? Type it in, and you'll get multiple options in seconds. Need a logo for your business that incorporates specific elements? Describe it, and the AI will generate options.

What are image generators being used for?

Marketing and advertising. Instead of hiring photographers or illustrators for every marketing campaign, businesses can use AI to generate images quickly and cheaply. This is both a threat and an opportunity. It's a threat to some traditional photographers and illustrators, but it's an opportunity for marketers and small business owners who couldn't afford professional visual content before.

A woman I know started a social media marketing business for small businesses in our community. She uses AI-generated images for her clients' social media posts. Her clients get professional-looking content at a fraction of what it would cost to hire a photographer for every post. And she built a business around this capability.

Concept art and design. Artists and designers use AI image generators to quickly explore visual concepts and ideas. Instead of spending hours sketching different options, they can generate dozens of variations in minutes, then refine the ones they like.

Educational materials. Teachers can generate images to illustrate concepts, create visual aids, or make learning materials more engaging without needing design skills or expensive stock photo subscriptions.

Personal projects. People use image generators for everything from creating custom art for their homes to designing invitations for events to generating character art for stories they're writing.

Product visualization. Businesses can generate images of products in different settings or with different features without needing physical prototypes or professional photo shoots.

Now, there are legitimate concerns about image generators. They raise questions about copyright (since they're trained on existing images), about artists' livelihoods, about the potential for creating misleading or harmful images, and about who owns the images that AI generates.

These are real issues that need to be addressed. But the technology exists, it's getting better, and it's being used. Ignoring it won't make it go away. Understanding it and figuring out how to use it ethically and effectively is the better strategy.

The opportunity here? Visual content is increasingly important in our digital world. If you can learn to use AI image generators effectively, you can create visual content for businesses, social media, education, marketing, or your own creative projects. You don't need years of art training or expensive equipment. You need creativity, an eye for what works visually, and the skills to write effective prompts that get the AI to generate what you're imagining.

Voice AI: Technology That Speaks and Listens

Voice AI has been around longer than you might think. Siri launched in 2011. But the quality and capabilities of voice AI have exploded in recent years.

Voice AI encompasses several different capabilities: speech recognition (turning spoken words into text), speech synthesis (turning text into spoken words), and voice assistants (AI that can understand and respond to voice commands).

Speech recognition and transcription. AI can now transcribe speech to text with remarkable accuracy. This is being used for everything from automatically generating captions for videos to transcribing meetings and interviews to enabling voice-to-text messaging.

A friend who's a journalist told me she uses AI transcription for every interview now. She records the conversation, runs it through an AI transcription service, and has a searchable text document of the entire interview within minutes. It used to take her hours to transcribe interviews manually. Now that part of her job is automated, freeing her up to focus on writing and analysis.

Voice assistants. Siri, Alexa, Google Assistant, and others use voice AI to understand spoken commands and respond appropriately. They're getting better at understanding context, handling follow-up questions, and completing complex tasks.

These assistants are particularly valuable for people with visual impairments or mobility limitations. Voice AI can make technology more accessible. But they're also just convenient for everyone. Setting timers while cooking, getting weather updates while getting dressed, controlling smart home devices while your hands are full. Voice AI makes all of this possible.

Voice cloning and synthesis. This is the newer and more controversial application. AI can now clone voices with high accuracy. This has legitimate uses (creating audiobooks, giving voice to people who've lost the ability to speak, generating voiceovers for videos) but it also has concerning implications (deepfakes, scams, impersonation).

A voice actor I spoke with was initially threatened by voice cloning technology. But then she realized she could license her voice for AI synthesis, getting paid for her voice to be used in projects without her having to spend hours in a recording booth. She's found a way to make the technology work for her rather than against her.

Call center automation. AI voice systems are increasingly handling customer service calls. They can understand questions, provide information, and even handle complaints. They're not perfect, and plenty of people still prefer talking to humans, but they're improving rapidly.

Language learning. Voice AI is being used to help people learn new languages by providing pronunciation feedback, conducting practice conversations, and offering instant corrections.

Accessibility. For people who have difficulty with traditional text-based interfaces, voice AI can make technology much more accessible. This is an important social benefit that sometimes gets overlooked in discussions about AI's economic impact.

The opportunity here? Voice AI is opening up

possibilities for content creation (audiobooks, podcasts, voiceovers), accessibility services, language services, customer service, and more. If you have a good voice, understanding voice AI might help you monetize that asset. If you have communication skills, voice AI tools might enhance your ability to serve clients or customers.

Recommendation Systems: The AI You Don't Notice

You probably interact with recommendation systems more than any other type of AI, but you might not think of them as AI because they work in the background.

Every time Netflix suggests a show, Spotify recommends a song, Amazon shows you products you might like, or Instagram decides what posts to put in your feed, that's a recommendation system powered by AI.

These systems work by analyzing massive amounts of data about what you and millions of other people have watched, listened to, bought, or engaged with. They find patterns in that data and use those patterns to predict what you'll be interested in next.

Think of it like having a friend who knows your taste really well and can suggest things you'll like. Except this "friend" has watched millions of people's behavior and can detect patterns no human could spot.

Why do recommendation systems matter?

They shape what we see. The content you're exposed to on social media, streaming services, shopping sites, and news platforms is largely determined by recommendation algorithms. This has huge implications for culture, politics, commerce, and society.

They influence purchasing decisions. Amazon's recommendation engine reportedly drives 35% of their sales. That's billions of dollars in purchases influenced by AI recommendations.

They affect what content gets made. Netflix decides what shows to produce based partly on what their recommendation algorithm says people want to watch. Musicians change their music based on what streaming algorithms favor. Content creators optimize their videos for YouTube's recommendation algorithm.

They create filter bubbles. By showing you more of what you've already shown interest in, recommendation algorithms can create echo chambers where you're not exposed to different viewpoints or new experiences. A woman I know who runs a small online boutique told me she had to learn how Instagram's recommendation algorithm works because it determines whether potential customers even see her posts. She's not selling to people scrolling through their feeds anymore. She's creating content that the algorithm will recognize as engaging so the algorithm will show her posts to more people. The algorithm is the gatekeeper.

The opportunity here? Understanding how recommendation systems work can help you in several ways. If you're a creator or business owner, you can optimize your content to work with these algorithms rather than against them. If you're a consumer, you can make more informed decisions about what you consume and how you're being influenced. And if you're ambitious, you could build businesses or services that help others navigate these algorithmic systems.

Autonomous Vehicles and Robotics: AI That Moves

Self-driving cars get a lot of attention in the media, and they're genuinely impressive examples of AI. But autonomous vehicles and robotics represent just one specific application of AI: using artificial intelligence to navigate physical space and manipulate physical objects.

Autonomous vehicles use AI to process information from cameras, sensors, and radar to understand their surroundings, predict what other vehicles and pedestrians will do, and make split-second decisions about acceleration, braking, and steering.

It's incredibly complex. The AI needs to identify objects (is that a person, a bicycle, or a mailbox?), predict motion (is that pedestrian about to step into the street?), understand context (those are construction cones, so I need to change lanes), and make safe decisions in constantly changing conditions.

Self-driving cars aren't fully here yet. We're still in a hybrid phase where cars have AI-assisted features like automatic emergency braking, lane-keeping assistance, and adaptive cruise control, but humans still need to be ready to take over.

But they're coming. And when they arrive at scale, they'll have enormous implications for employment (truck drivers, delivery drivers, taxi drivers), for urban planning (fewer parking lots needed if self-driving cars can drop you off and go park themselves elsewhere), and for accessibility (people who can't drive due to age, disability, or other factors will have more mobility options).

Beyond cars, robotics powered by AI is advancing in warehouses (Amazon's fulfillment centers use thousands of robots), manufacturing (AI-powered robots are more flexible than traditional industrial robots), agriculture (robots that can identify and pick ripe fruit), and even homes (robot vacuums, lawn mowers, and more sophisticated home robots in development).

A cousin who works in a warehouse told me they brought in robots a few years ago and everyone was terrified they'd lose their jobs. But what actually happened was the robots took over the most physically demanding and repetitive tasks (moving heavy pallets around), while the human workers were retrained to handle tasks requiring judgment, flexibility, and problem-solving. The robots didn't replace the humans. They changed what the humans did.

That's not always how it goes. Some jobs are being eliminated by automation. But it's a reminder that the future isn't necessarily "robots replace all humans." Sometimes it's "robots and humans work together, each doing what they do best."

The opportunity here? Robotics and autonomous systems need human workers to maintain them, program them, supervise them, and handle exceptions. These are skilled jobs that pay well. But they require training. If you're interested in working with physical technology, understanding how AI powers these systems could lead to career opportunities.

AI in Healthcare: Diagnosing and Treating

AI is transforming healthcare in multiple ways, and this is one area where the technology is already saving lives.

Medical imaging analysis. AI is excellent at analyzing X-rays, MRIs, CT scans, and other medical images. It's been trained on millions of images to identify patterns associated with diseases like cancer, heart disease, and neurological conditions. In some cases, AI can spot things human doctors miss.

A doctor I spoke with at a health fair said he initially resisted AI diagnostic tools because he trusted his own expertise. But after a case where the AI caught a small tumor he'd overlooked, he changed his mind. Now he sees AI as a second set of eyes, helping him catch things earlier and make more accurate diagnoses.

This doesn't mean AI is replacing doctors. But it's becoming a tool doctors use to be more effective.

Drug discovery. Developing new drugs traditionally takes over a decade and costs billions of dollars. AI is speeding this up by analyzing molecular structures and predicting which compounds might work against specific diseases. Several drugs discovered with AI assistance are now in clinical trials.

Personalized treatment. AI can analyze a patient's genetic information, medical history, lifestyle factors, and more to help predict which treatments will be most effective for that specific person. This is the promise of personalized medicine, and AI is making it possible at scale.

Administrative tasks. A huge amount of healthcare

work is paperwork. AI is being used to automate scheduling, billing, insurance claims, medical record documentation, and other administrative tasks. This frees up healthcare workers to spend more time with patients.

Mental health support. AI-powered chatbots are being used to provide mental health support, offering coping strategies, checking in on people's emotional state, and even detecting warning signs of crises. They're not replacing therapists, but they're providing accessible support for people who might not otherwise have access to mental health services.

Predictive healthcare. AI can analyze health data to predict who's at risk for conditions like diabetes, heart disease, or stroke. This allows for early intervention before problems become severe.

Here's why this matters for our community: healthcare disparities are real. Black Americans have worse health outcomes than white Americans for a wide range of conditions. Part of this is due to unequal access to healthcare, but part of it is also due to biases in medical training and treatment.

AI could help reduce some of these disparities if it's trained on diverse data and designed with equity in mind. But it could also make them worse if the AI is trained primarily on data from white patients.

Who builds these AI systems and what data they're trained on matters enormously for health equity.

The opportunity here? Healthcare is one of the fastest-growing sectors, and it's integrating AI throughout. Jobs in health informatics, medical AI, healthcare technology, and related fields are growing. If you're interested in healthcare and technology, this intersection is full of opportunity. And if you're already in healthcare, understanding AI could help you stay competitive and provide better care.

AI in Finance: Money and Algorithms

Finance has been using AI longer than most industries, and it's deeply integrated throughout the financial system.

Fraud detection. Every time you use your credit card, AI is analyzing that transaction in real-time to determine if it's legitimate or potentially fraudulent. The AI learned patterns of normal spending behavior and can flag anomalies that might indicate theft or fraud.

A friend had her card information stolen last year. She didn't notice. But her bank's AI system flagged unusual purchases within minutes and froze her account before significant damage was done. That AI potentially saved her thousands of dollars.

Credit scoring and loan approval. Banks use AI to assess credit risk and make decisions about loan approvals. This has benefits (faster decisions, the ability to consider factors beyond traditional credit scores) but also risks (potential for bias if the AI was trained on historical data that reflects past discrimination).

Algorithmic trading. A huge percentage of stock trading is now done by AI algorithms that can execute trades in milliseconds based on market conditions. These algorithms analyze news, social media, price movements, and thousands of other factors to make split-second trading decisions.

Personalized financial advice. AI-powered

robo-advisors can provide investment recommendations based on your financial goals, risk tolerance, and current situation. They're making financial planning more accessible to people who couldn't afford traditional financial advisors.

Insurance pricing. Insurance companies use AI to assess risk and set premiums. The AI analyzes driving records, health information, property data, and other factors to predict the likelihood of claims.

Customer service. Banks and financial institutions use AI chatbots to answer questions, help with transactions, and provide account information. This allows 24/7 customer service at lower cost than staffing human representatives around the clock.

Here's what concerns me about AI in finance: these systems are making decisions that profoundly affect people's lives (can you get a loan to buy a house? what interest rate will you pay? can you get insurance?), but often the people being affected don't understand how the decisions are being made or have any ability to challenge them if they're wrong.

And there's evidence that some AI systems in finance replicate historical biases. If an AI is trained on decades of loan data that reflects discriminatory lending practices, it might learn to discriminate even without being explicitly programmed to do so.

This is why we need people from our community involved in building and overseeing these systems. To make sure they're fair. To advocate for transparency. To push back when AI systems perpetuate discrimination.

The opportunity here? Finance technology (fintech) is

booming. Jobs in financial AI, risk analysis, fraud detection, and related fields are plentiful. If you have financial skills or interest, learning about AI in finance could open doors. And if you're entrepreneurial, there are opportunities to build fintech services that serve underserved communities.

AI in Law: Research, Analysis, and Prediction

The legal profession is being transformed by AI, though most people don't realize it because the changes are happening behind the scenes.

Legal research. Lawyers used to spend hours searching through case law to find relevant precedents. AI can now search through millions of legal documents in seconds and identify the most relevant cases. This dramatically speeds up legal research.

A lawyer I know told me AI legal research tools have made her much more efficient. She can take on more clients and provide better service because she's not spending all her time on research. The AI does the initial search, she reviews the results and applies her legal judgment.

Document review. In large legal cases, there might be millions of documents to review. AI can analyze documents to identify which ones are relevant, flag potential issues, and even predict which documents the opposing side is likely to focus on. This task used to require armies of junior lawyers working around the clock. Now AI can do it faster and cheaper.

Contract analysis. AI can review contracts to identify key terms, flag unusual clauses, spot potential problems, and even suggest standard language. This is useful for businesses that need to review many contracts.

Predictive analytics. AI can analyze past cases to predict outcomes of current cases. It can estimate the likelihood of winning or losing, the potential damages or settlement amounts, and which legal strategies are most likely to succeed. This helps lawyers advise clients and make strategic decisions.

Access to justice. AI-powered legal chatbots can provide basic legal information to people who can't afford lawyers. They can't replace lawyers for complex cases, but they can help people understand their rights and navigate simple legal processes.

The concerns here are similar to other fields: AI might reduce demand for some legal jobs (particularly junior lawyers who used to do document review), the AI might have biases in how it analyzes cases, and there are questions about whether AI predictions should influence legal outcomes.

But the potential benefits are also significant. AI could make legal services more affordable and accessible. It could help reduce the backlog of cases in the court system. It could help people without lawyers understand their legal options.

The opportunity here? Legal technology is a growing field. If you're interested in law and technology, this is an area to watch. Paralegals, legal researchers, and others who work in law need to understand how AI is changing their field. And there are opportunities to build legal tech tools that serve communities that have historically had limited access to legal services.

Each Type Represents Different Opportunities

Here's what I want you to understand from this chapter: AI isn't one thing. It's many different technologies with different capabilities, different applications, and different implications.

When someone says "AI is going to take all our jobs," they're oversimplifying. Some types of AI will eliminate some jobs. Other types will create new jobs. Many types will change jobs, requiring different skills but not eliminating the need for human workers.

When someone says "AI is the future," they need to be more specific. Which type of AI? For what purpose? With what implications?

The key is to understand the different types so you can identify which ones are relevant to your life and your goals. Are you in healthcare? You need to understand AI in medical imaging and diagnostics. Are you in marketing? You need to understand image generators and language models. Are you in customer service? You need to understand chatbots and voice AI. Are you creative? You need to understand the AI tools that can enhance your creativity. Are you entrepreneurial? You need to identify gaps where AI could solve problems in your community.

Every type of AI we discussed in this chapter represents opportunities. Jobs that need to be done. Problems that need to be solved. Services that could be provided. Businesses that could be built.

But you can only spot those opportunities if you understand what the different types of AI can do.

An entrepreneur I met last year started a business helping small Black-owned businesses use AI tools. She learned about language models, image generators, and other AI technologies. Then she packaged that knowledge into a service. She helps businesses write better marketing copy, create visual content, automate customer service, and more. She's not building AI. She's helping others use AI effectively. And she built a thriving business doing it.

That's one example. There are thousands of other opportunities across all the different types of AI we discussed. The question isn't whether AI is going to change things. It already is.

The question is whether you're going to understand it well enough to benefit from those changes.

In the next chapter, we're going to talk about something crucial: how AI is already changing the job market right now. Not in some distant future. Today. And why that should terrify you into action if nothing else has.

Let's get real about what's happening to jobs in the age of AI.

CHAPTER FOUR

AI IS ALREADY CHANGING YOUR JOB

I need you to understand something that a lot of people are still in denial about: AI isn't coming for jobs in the future. It's taking them right now. Today. While you're reading this sentence, someone somewhere is being told their position has been eliminated because AI can do it cheaper and faster.

This isn't speculation. This isn't fear-mongering. This is what's actually happening.

A woman I met at a workshop last month worked in customer service for a major telecommunications company for eight years. Good employee. Never missed work. Knew the products inside and out. Customers loved her. Last December, she and thirty-seven other customer service reps got called into a meeting and told their positions were being eliminated. The company was implementing an AI chatbot system that could handle 80% of the inquiries they used to handle.

They offered her a severance package and job placement assistance. She's 52 years old. She's been applying for jobs for four months. Most companies in her field are doing the same thing her old company did. They're replacing human customer service reps with AI.

She told me, with tears in her eyes, "I thought I had another fifteen years until retirement. Now I don't know what I'm going to do."

That conversation haunts me because I know she's not alone. I know there are thousands, maybe hundreds of thousands, of people in similar situations. And millions more who don't realize they're next.

This chapter is going to be uncomfortable. I'm going to show you exactly which jobs are being eliminated, which industries are being disrupted, and why our community is particularly vulnerable. I'm not doing this to scare you. I'm doing it because you need to know what you're up against.

You can't prepare for something you don't see coming. And too many people still don't see this coming.

The Jobs Disappearing Right Now

Let me be specific about which jobs are being eliminated by AI right this minute.

Customer Service Representatives. This is the big one. Chatbots powered by language models can now handle a huge percentage of customer service interactions. They can answer questions, process returns, troubleshoot problems, and even handle complaints. They work 24/7, never get tired, never get frustrated, and cost a fraction of what human workers cost.

IBM announced in 2023 that they were pausing hiring for back-office roles that could be replaced by AI, estimating that 7,800 jobs could eventually be replaced. Klarna, a financial services company, reported in 2024 that their AI assistant was doing the work of 700 full-time customer service agents. Let that sink in. One AI system replaced 700 people.

Is AI as good as the best human customer service reps? No. But it's good enough for most routine interactions, and it's getting better every month. Companies don't need AI to be perfect. They just need it to be good enough and cheap enough to justify eliminating human positions.

Data Entry Clerks. AI can extract information from documents, invoices, forms, and other sources and enter it into databases faster and more accurately than humans. This used to be a reliable entry-level job for people without college degrees. Those jobs are disappearing rapidly.

A man I spoke with worked data entry for a medical billing company. In 2022, his department had twenty employees. Today it has six. The company implemented AI software that processes claims automatically. The remaining employees just review the AI's work and handle exceptions.

Telemarketers and Cold Callers. AI voice systems can now make sales calls that sound remarkably human. They can handle objections, answer questions, and even close sales. And they can make thousands of calls simultaneously without getting discouraged by rejection.

Basic Bookkeeping and Accounting. AI can categorize expenses, generate financial reports, flag discrepancies, and handle routine accounting tasks that used to require human accountants. Bookkeepers who only do basic transaction recording are being squeezed out. The accountants who survive are the ones who can do higher-level analysis and strategic financial planning that AI can't handle yet.

Retail Cashiers. Self-checkout systems have already reduced the need for cashiers, but AI is taking it further. Amazon Go stores have no checkout at all. Cameras and sensors track what you take, and you're automatically charged when you leave. Other retailers are testing similar systems.

Assembly Line Workers. Manufacturing has been automating for decades, but AI-powered robots are more flexible and capable than previous generations of automation. They can handle more complex tasks and adapt to different products without being completely reprogrammed.

Transcriptionists. AI can now transcribe audio to text with over 90% accuracy. Court reporters, medical transcriptionists, and others who transcribed audio for a living are seeing their work dry up.

Travel Agents. Most people already book their own travel online, but AI is finishing off the few remaining travel agents by providing personalized recommendations and handling complex itineraries automatically.

Loan Officers and Underwriters. AI algorithms now make most lending decisions. They evaluate credit risk, verify information, and approve or deny loans with minimal human involvement. The loan officers who remain mostly just explain decisions the AI already made.

A man who had worked as a loan processor for fifteen years told me his job changed completely in the last three years. He used to evaluate applications and make judgment calls based on the full picture of someone's financial situation.

Now the AI makes the decision. He just enters information and communicates what the AI decided. He went from being a decision-maker to being an interface between humans and the algorithm.

He hates it. But he's grateful he still has a job. Half his department was laid off.

Warehouse Workers. Amazon and other companies use robots to move products around warehouses. Fewer human workers are needed to do the same amount of work. The humans who remain are often managed by AI systems that track their productivity and assign them tasks.

Drivers (Eventually). This one hasn't fully hit yet, but it's coming. When self-driving vehicles become reliable enough to operate without human supervision, millions of truck drivers, taxi drivers, delivery drivers, and bus drivers will be at risk. Some estimates suggest this could happen within the next decade.

These aren't the only jobs being affected. These are just the ones where the impact is already clearly visible. And this is just the beginning.

Industries Being Disrupted Right Now

Beyond specific jobs, entire industries are being transformed by AI. Let me show you what's happening in a few key sectors.

Journalism and Media.

News organizations are using AI to write articles. Sports scores, financial reports, weather updates, and other routine stories are increasingly written by AI. The Associated Press has been using AI to write corporate earnings reports since 2014. Dozens of other news organizations have followed.

Is AI going to replace investigative journalists who break major stories? Probably not. But it's already replacing reporters who write routine stories. And it's putting pressure on all journalists to produce more content faster because they're competing against AI that can pump out articles in seconds.

A journalist I know watched his newsroom shrink by 40% over the last five years. The reporters who survived are the ones who can do things AI can't: build sources, conduct in-depth investigations, provide local expertise and context, and write with a distinctive voice. The reporters who just rewrote press releases or covered routine events? Most of them are gone.

The newspaper industry has been struggling for years due to declining print revenue. AI is accelerating the decline by making it possible to produce content with fewer human journalists.

Graphic Design and Visual Arts.

AI image generators are disrupting the entire visual content industry. Stock photo companies are seeing their business model threatened because AI can generate custom images on demand. Graphic designers who produce routine marketing materials are competing with clients who can now generate their own images for free.

An illustrator I spoke with said she used to get steady work creating custom illustrations for articles, blog posts, and marketing materials. That work has dried up. Now she focuses on high-end work where clients specifically want a human artist's style and vision. But there's much less of that work, and far more competition for it.

Book cover designers, logo designers, social media content creators, and others who work in visual content are all feeling the pressure. The designers who are surviving are the ones who've learned to use AI as a tool in their workflow or who've specialized in work that requires human creativity and judgment.

Accounting and Tax Preparation.

AI can now handle a huge percentage of what accountants used to do. Small business bookkeeping, personal tax returns, payroll processing, expense categorization and basic financial reporting. All of this can be done by AI with minimal human supervision.

H&R Block, TurboTax, and other tax software companies have been using AI for years. But now AI is sophisticated enough to handle more complex situations that used to require a human CPA.

A CPA told me his firm used to have five junior accountants who did basic tax returns and bookkeeping. Now they have one, and that person mainly reviews the work AI does automatically. The firm's revenue hasn't dropped because they're serving the same number of clients. But they're doing it with far fewer employees.

Accountants who survive and thrive are the ones providing strategic financial advice, tax strategy, financial planning, and other services that require human judgment and deep expertise.

Legal Services.

As we discussed in the last chapter, AI is transforming legal work. Document review, legal research, contract analysis, and even predicting case outcomes can now be done by AI. Large law firms have cut hundreds of junior attorney positions because AI can do the work those attorneys used to do. A junior lawyer used to spend years reviewing documents and doing legal research. Now AI does that in minutes.

This is creating a crisis in the legal profession. Law schools are still producing the same number of graduates, but there are fewer entry-level positions. Young lawyers can't get the experience they need because the entry-level work has been automated.

A lawyer told me that when she started practicing in the late 1990s, every large case required dozens of junior attorneys to review documents. Now one senior attorney with AI tools can do what used to take twenty people.

Advertising and Marketing.

AI can now generate ad copy, create visual ads, optimize campaigns, target audiences, and measure results with minimal human involvement. Small businesses that used to hire marketing agencies are now using AI tools to do their own marketing.

A marketing consultant said she's had to completely reinvent her business. She can't just offer to write ad copy or design social media graphics anymore because clients can get that from AI for free. Now she focuses on strategy, brand development, and campaign planning; the things that still require human insight and creativity.

Education and Tutoring.

AI tutors can provide personalized instruction in math, science, languages, and other subjects. They can adapt to each student's learning pace and style. They never get impatient or tired. And they cost a fraction of what human tutors charge.

This doesn't mean teachers are being replaced. But tutors, test prep instructors, and others who provide supplemental education are facing competition from AI alternatives that are good enough and much cheaper.

Healthcare Administration.

Medical billing, appointment scheduling, insurance verification, booking, medical record documentation are all administrative tasks that employ hundreds of thousands of people in healthcare are increasingly being automated by AI.

A medical office manager told me her office used to employ three people just to handle billing and insurance. Now they have one person who oversees AI software that does most of it automatically. The two positions they eliminated? They didn't replace them when those employees retired.

The pattern is clear: industries across the economy are using AI to reduce headcount. Some companies are replacing workers directly. Others are just not filling positions when people leave or retire. Either way, there are fewer jobs for humans.

Jobs in Our Community Most at Risk

Now let me talk about something that makes me angry and should make you angry too: the jobs being eliminated by

AI are disproportionately held by Black workers.

This isn't accidental. This is the pattern playing out again. According to research from the Brookings Institution and other economic think tanks, Black workers are more likely than white workers to be in occupations that are highly exposed to automation and AI replacement.

Let me give you specific numbers:

Customer service representatives: Black workers make up about 17% of customer service reps, higher than our 13% share of the overall workforce. And as we've already discussed, customer service is one of the jobs being most aggressively automated.

Data entry workers: Black workers are overrepresented in data entry and administrative support roles and these are exactly the roles that AI can easily replace.

Retail workers: Black workers make up about 12% of retail workers, and we're more likely to work as cashiers and in other front-line roles that are vulnerable to automation.

Food service workers: We're overrepresented in fast food and food service, industries that are rapidly automating with self-service kiosks and AI ordering systems.

Transportation and warehousing: Black workers make up about 17% of workers in transportation and warehousing, industries that will be heavily impacted by autonomous vehicles and warehouse robots.

Office and administrative support: We're overrepresented in administrative and clerical roles that AI is eliminating.

Do you see the pattern? We're concentrated in exactly the jobs that AI is coming for first.

Meanwhile, Black workers are significantly underrepresented in the jobs that are most likely to survive and thrive in the AI era: computer science, engineering, data analysis, AI development, and other technical roles.

A study by McKinsey estimated that Black workers are 10% more likely to need to change occupations by 2030 due to automation than white workers. Ten percent might not sound like a lot, but when you're talking about millions of jobs, that's a massive disparity.

And here's what makes it worse: when workers are displaced by automation, white workers generally have an easier time transitioning to new careers. They have better access to education and training programs. They have stronger professional networks. They're more likely to have savings to fall back on during a job transition. They face less discrimination in hiring.

All of these factors that already make economic mobility harder for Black workers are going to be amplified as AI disrupts the job market.

A workforce development specialist I spoke with runs a program helping displaced workers retrain for new careers. She told me that the Black workers in her program face extra challenges. They're more likely to be supporting extended family, so they can't easily take time off for training. They're less likely to have college degrees, which some training programs require. They face discrimination when they apply for jobs in new fields. And they have less margin for error because they have less savings to fall back on if the transition doesn't work out.

She's seeing people fall through the cracks. Good workers. Smart, capable people. But they got displaced from jobs that don't exist anymore, and they're struggling to find their footing in a rapidly changing economy.

This is the reality. AI is hitting our community harder than it's hitting other communities. And most people in our community don't even realize it's happening yet.

Real Numbers You Need to Know

Let me hit you with some statistics that should wake you up if you're not already alarmed.

Job displacement projections: McKinsey estimates that by 2030, up to 375 million workers globally may need to switch occupations due to automation and AI. In the United States, that could be as many as 30% of workers.

AI adoption rate: A 2024 survey found that 65% of organizations are regularly using AI, up from just 20% in 2017. This adoption is accelerating, not slowing down.

Productivity gains: Companies using AI are reporting 20-40% productivity increases. That sounds good until you realize that increased productivity with the same amount of work means fewer workers needed.

Hiring freezes: Multiple major companies have announced hiring freezes or slowdowns for roles that AI can perform. IBM, as mentioned earlier, paused hiring for roles they believe AI can do. Dropbox announced they would be more selective in hiring because AI tools made their existing workforce more productive.

Income replacement: The World Economic Forum estimates that while AI will eliminate 85 million jobs globally, it may also create 97 million new jobs. That sounds optimistic until you realize two things: First, the people losing jobs aren't necessarily the people who will get the new jobs. The new jobs require different skills. Second, the new jobs don't necessarily pay as well as the jobs being eliminated.

Wage pressure: Even workers who keep their jobs are seeing wage pressure. Why should a company pay higher wages when they can credibly threaten to replace workers with AI? This is already happening in fields like journalism, graphic design, and writing where workers are being told to accept lower rates because they're competing with AI.

Investment in AI: Companies invested over $200 billion in AI in 2024, and that number is expected to grow. That money isn't being invested out of curiosity. Companies expect returns on that investment, primarily through increased efficiency (which means fewer workers needed) and new capabilities.

Speed of change: Here's what's terrifying: the pace of AI advancement is accelerating. ChatGPT went from barely usable to genuinely impressive in less than two years. Image generators went from producing obviously fake images to near-photorealistic results in about a year. Voice AI went from robotic to natural-sounding in months.

Every few months, AI capabilities leap forward. And every time AI gets more capable, more jobs become automatable.

A technology analyst I spoke with said something that stuck with me: "We used to think technological change happened gradually, giving workers time to adapt. But AI isn't gradual. It's punctuated. For years nothing much happens, then suddenly there's a breakthrough, and within months the job market in an entire field can be transformed."

That's what we're seeing. And it's happening faster than our institutions (schools, training programs, government safety nets) can adapt.

Companies Already Reducing Headcount

Let me be concrete about companies that are already using AI to eliminate positions.

Duolingo: In 2024, Duolingo laid off contractors who were translating and creating educational content. They replaced them with AI. The CEO openly said AI was allowing them to be more efficient with fewer people.

Chegg: The online education company saw its stock collapse and announced layoffs in 2024 because students were using ChatGPT instead of paying for Chegg's services. This is an entire business model being disrupted by AI.

IBM: As mentioned, they've essentially stopped hiring for back-office roles they believe AI can do.

UPS: Announced plans to reduce their workforce and cited increased automation and AI-driven route optimization as factors allowing them to operate with fewer workers.

Google: Despite being one of the leaders in AI development, Google announced layoffs in 2024, explicitly stating that AI would allow them to operate more efficiently with fewer employees.

Meta: Same story. Laid off thousands of workers and said AI would allow remaining workers to be more productive. Microsoft: Laid off workers in customer service and support roles, replacing them with AI systems.

Goldman Sachs: Estimated that AI could replace the equivalent of 300 million full-time jobs globally, and they're preparing for that future by investing heavily in AI for their own operations.

Teleperformance: One of the world's largest call center companies announced they would be reducing headcount by using AI to handle customer service interactions.

These aren't struggling companies trying to survive. These are profitable corporations choosing to use AI to reduce labor costs and increase profit margins.

And here's the pattern: when companies announce layoffs due to AI, their stock prices often go up. The market rewards companies for cutting labor costs. This creates pressure on every company to find ways to reduce headcount.

A former HR director told me that in executive meetings she attended, there was explicit discussion of "right-sizing" the workforce by identifying roles that could be automated. They didn't see it as firing people. They saw it as optimizing operations. The people losing their jobs were just numbers on a spreadsheet. Cost savings to be realized.

That's the reality. You're not a person to these companies. You're a line item. And if AI can do your job for less money, they'll replace you.

This Is Happening Right Now

I need to hammer this point home because I still meet people who think AI job displacement is something that might happen in the future.

It's happening now.

Right now, someone is being told their job is being eliminated because of AI.

Right now, a company is deciding not to fill an open position because AI can do the work.

Right now, someone is accepting lower wages because they're competing with AI.

Right now, a college graduate is discovering that the entry-level jobs they expected to get don't exist anymore because AI does that work now.

This isn't theoretical. This isn't something to worry about someday. This is the current reality.

A career counselor told me she's seeing young people graduate with degrees in fields where jobs are evaporating. Graphic design graduates discovering that most companies now use AI for design work. Journalism graduates finding that news organizations are hiring fewer reporters. Business graduates learning that many entry-level business roles have been automated.

These young people did everything right. They went to school. They got degrees. They developed skills. And the job market changed before they even entered it.

That's what makes this crisis different from previous

economic disruptions. It's not just affecting older workers who can retire soon. It's affecting young people at the start of their careers. It's affecting mid-career workers who thought they had job security. It's affecting everyone who assumed their skills would always be valuable.

An economics professor I talked to put it this way: "Previous technological revolutions created more jobs than they destroyed. But they did it over decades, giving workers time to adapt. AI is different. It's affecting white-collar and blue-collar jobs simultaneously. It's moving faster than previous technological changes. And we're not certain it will create as many good jobs as it destroys."

That uncertainty is terrifying. Because what if this time is different? What if AI eliminates more jobs than it creates? What if the new jobs it creates don't pay as well as the jobs it's eliminating? What if most people can't transition to the new jobs because they require skills that take years to develop?

These aren't crazy questions. These are the questions economists are genuinely debating right now.

The Wake-Up Call

Here's what I need you to understand: the time to prepare was yesterday. The second-best time is right now.
If you're in a job that involves routine, predictable tasks, you need to be thinking about how AI might affect your role.

If you're in a job where you basically follow a script or standard procedures, you need to be developing skills that are harder to automate.

If you're in a job where you could theoretically train

someone to do it in a few weeks or months, that job is at risk.

If you're planning to enter a field where entry-level positions are being automated, you need to reconsider your plan.

I'm not saying this to scare you into paralysis. I'm saying this to motivate you to action.

A man I met at a community center summed it up well. He said, "I spent twenty years being comfortable. I had a steady job. It paid decent. I didn't worry about the future. Then one day they told me I was being laid off because AI could do my job. Now I'm starting over at 47, competing for jobs with people half my age. I wish someone had warned me this was coming. I would have prepared."

That's why I'm writing this book. That's why this chapter is so direct and uncomfortable. Because I don't want you to be that person at 47, wishing someone had warned you.

You're being warned now.

The question is: what are you going to do about it?

In the next chapter, we're going to talk about the jobs that are being created by AI. Because it's not all doom and gloom. There are opportunities. But those opportunities go to people who are prepared, who have the right skills, and who move fast.

The jobs being eliminated aren't being replaced one-to-one with equivalent jobs. But new opportunities are emerging. Different opportunities. Better opportunities in some cases, but only for people who are ready for them.

Are you ready?

If not, it's time to get ready.
Because the workplace transformation isn't coming.
It's already here.

CHAPTER FIVE

THE NEW JOBS BEING CREATED

Alright, I know the last chapter was heavy. I showed you all the jobs being eliminated, all the ways AI is disrupting employment, all the reasons to be concerned about the future of work.

But here's what I need you to understand: while one door is closing, another door is opening. A bigger door. A door leading to opportunities that didn't exist five years ago. Opportunities that pay better than the jobs being eliminated. Opportunities that don't necessarily require a four-year degree or decades of experience.

But that door won't stay open forever. Right now, we're in the early stages of the AI revolution. Companies desperately need people with AI skills. They're paying premium wages. They're willing to hire people without traditional credentials if they can demonstrate capability. They're creating entirely new job categories because the work needs to be done and there aren't enough qualified people to do it.

This is the opportunity. This is the moment.

But it's not going to last. As more people develop AI skills, competition will increase. As educational institutions catch up and start producing graduates with AI training, the premium for these skills will decrease. As the field matures, requirements will become more rigid and pathways to entry will narrow.

I talked to a woman who got into web development in the mid-1990s. She taught herself HTML and basic web design from library books. Back then, companies were so desperate for anyone who could build websites that they'd hire people with barely any experience and train them on the job. She built an entire career from that early start. Today, she runs a successful web development agency.

But if she were starting today? She'd be competing against thousands of boot camp graduates and computer science degree holders. The barrier to entry is much higher now. The early advantage is gone.

That's where we are with AI right now. We're in the 1990s of the AI revolution. The people who move now, who develop skills now, who position themselves now, they're going to have advantages that latecomers won't have.

So let's talk about where the opportunities are.

The Jobs That Didn't Exist Five Years Ago

Let me start by listing actual job titles that barely existed in 2020 but are now in high demand:

AI Prompt Engineer. This is someone who knows how to communicate effectively with AI systems to get the best results. They understand how to write prompts that produce high-quality outputs from language models. They know how to troubleshoot when the AI isn't giving good results. They understand the capabilities and limitations of different AI systems.

When ChatGPT exploded onto the scene in late 2022, suddenly everyone needed prompt engineers. Companies realized that knowing how to effectively interact with AI was a valuable skill. People who figured out prompt engineering early were getting hired for six-figure salaries.

A guy I met at a tech conference taught himself prompt engineering in his spare time while working a retail job. He practiced with ChatGPT, documented techniques that worked, built a portfolio of examples, and within six months had landed a remote job as a prompt engineer making $95,000 a year. He had no degree, no prior tech experience. Just skills he taught himself and the hustle to prove he had them.

AI Trainer. These are people who train AI systems by providing feedback on AI outputs, labeling data, and helping AI learn to perform specific tasks. It's like being a teacher for AI. The work varies from simple (rating which AI response is better) to complex (explaining nuanced judgments about quality, appropriateness, and accuracy).

The pay for AI training work ranges from modest for simple tasks to substantial for specialized knowledge. If you have expertise in a particular field (medicine, law, engineering, languages, culture), you can make good money training AI systems in that domain.

A retired teacher I know does AI training part-time, helping language models learn to explain educational concepts more effectively. She works from home, sets her own hours, and makes $40 per hour. It's not replacing a full-time income, but it's excellent supplemental money for work that's actually engaging.

AI Ethics Specialist. As concerns about AI bias, fairness, transparency, and accountability have grown, companies need people who can evaluate AI systems for ethical issues and ensure they're being used responsibly.

This role requires understanding both the technical side (how AI works) and the human side (ethical frameworks, social impact, fairness considerations). It's a new field, so there's no standard credential. People come to it from philosophy, sociology, law, computer science, and other backgrounds.

AI Product Manager. Someone who understands both AI capabilities and business needs, who can identify opportunities to use AI, manage AI development projects, and ensure AI products actually solve real problems.

Machine Learning Operations (MLOps) Engineer. These are people who manage the infrastructure and workflows for deploying and maintaining AI systems. They make sure AI models are running smoothly, being updated properly, and integrated correctly with other systems.

AI Content Creator. People who use AI tools to create content more efficiently. This includes writers who use AI writing assistants, designers who use AI image generators, video creators who use AI video tools, and others who've learned to leverage AI to dramatically increase their productivity. A content creator I spoke with produces social media content for small businesses. She used to be able to handle maybe five clients doing everything manually. Now, using AI tools for image generation, caption writing, and content scheduling, she handles twenty clients. Her income quadrupled because she can serve more clients in the same amount of time.

AI Integration Consultant. Companies know they need to use AI but don't know how. They need consultants who can assess their operations, identify opportunities for AI integration, recommend solutions, and help implement them. This is entrepreneurial work. You're helping businesses transform how they operate.

Conversational AI Designer. People who design how chatbots and voice assistants interact with users. They create the conversation flows, write the responses, and make sure the AI interactions feel natural and helpful.

Synthetic Data Engineer. As privacy concerns grow and real data becomes harder to obtain, companies need people who can create realistic synthetic data for training AI systems.

AI Policy Analyst. Governments and organizations need people who understand AI well enough to help create policies and regulations around its use. This is particularly important for ensuring AI is used fairly and doesn't perpetuate discrimination.

These are just some of the new roles. The field is moving so fast that new job categories are emerging constantly. The Bureau of Labor Statistics can't even keep up with categorizing all the new roles because they're evolving faster than government bureaucracy can document them.

An employment researcher told me that by her estimate,

there are at least fifty distinct AI-related job categories that didn't exist in 2019. And within each category, there are multiple specializations and variations.

This is a rapidly expanding field. The opportunities are real. But you have to know they exist and you have to position yourself to take advantage of them.

The Skills That Are Paying Premium Wages

Let's talk about money, because that's what makes this opportunity real for most people.

Workers with AI skills are making significantly more than workers without AI skills in comparable roles. The numbers are striking.

According to multiple salary surveys and reports:

AI Engineers and Machine Learning Specialists are averaging $120,000 to $180,000 in the United States, with senior roles paying $200,000 to $300,000 or more. These are the people building AI systems from scratch, requiring strong technical skills in programming, mathematics, and computer science.

AI Prompt Engineers are making $80,000 to $150,000, depending on specialization and experience. This is remarkable because the role barely existed two years ago, and you don't necessarily need a computer science degree to do it.

AI Integration Specialists and Consultants are charging $100 to $300 per hour, or taking full-time positions at $90,000 to $150,000. This role is about understanding both AI and business, not necessarily about building AI from scratch.

AI Trainers with specialized knowledge are making $50 to $100 per hour, with some specialized roles paying even more. A medical professional who trains AI systems to understand medical terminology and concepts can command premium rates.

Regular workers who add AI skills are seeing salary increases of 40% to 60%. A marketing professional who learns to use AI tools effectively can command significantly higher pay than a marketer without those skills. A writer who uses AI tools to increase productivity and output can charge more or take on more clients. A designer who integrates AI into their workflow becomes more valuable.

Let me give you concrete examples of this pay premium:

A copywriter I know was making $50,000 per year writing marketing content the traditional way. She learned to use AI writing tools effectively. Now she's making $85,000 doing similar work but producing it three times faster. The AI didn't replace her. It made her more valuable because she can deliver more value to clients in less time.

A data analyst who added AI and machine learning skills to his resume saw his salary jump from $65,000 to $110,000 within eighteen months. Same industry, similar type of work, but the AI skills made him far more valuable.

A customer service manager learned how to implement and manage AI chatbot systems. She went from making $55,000 as a regular customer service manager to $95,000 as an AI customer experience manager. The role is similar, overseeing customer service, but now she's also managing AI systems, and that skill commands a premium.

This pay gap exists because demand is outpacing supply. Companies need these skills more than there are people who have them. Basic economics: when something is in high demand and low supply, the price goes up.

But this won't last forever. As more people develop AI skills, the supply will increase and the premium will shrink. The people getting in now are capturing the value of being early. The people who wait will find the opportunity has become more competitive and less lucrative.

A tech recruiter told me that three years ago, if someone had legitimate AI skills on their resume, they'd get interview requests from multiple companies within days of posting their resume online. Today, it's still in demand, but less dramatic. In another three years? It'll probably be a standard expected skill, not a premium differentiator.

The time to capture the premium is now.

Remote Work Opportunities Are Exploding

Here's another massive advantage of AI-related work: much of it can be done remotely.

You don't need to live in San Francisco or New York or Seattle to access these opportunities. You can work from anywhere with a decent internet connection.

This is huge for our community. Historically, many high-paying tech jobs required relocating to expensive cities where cost of living ate up much of the salary premium. But AI work often doesn't require you to be in an office.

A woman I know lives in a small town in Alabama. Cost

of living is low. She works remotely as an AI prompt engineer for a company based in California. She makes $105,000 per year. In her town, that salary goes much further than it would in California. She's building wealth in a way that would be impossible if she had to relocate to access that salary.

Remote work also means you're not competing just with local job seekers. You're competing globally. But it also means you have access to opportunities globally. For someone with the right skills, the entire world becomes your potential job market.

A young man I spoke with does AI training work for multiple companies simultaneously. He lives in Atlanta but works for clients in three different countries. He pieces together income from various sources, making about $90,000 per year total. None of his clients care where he lives. They care that he does quality work.

This is the future of work: skills-based, remote, flexible. AI work is at the forefront of this trend.

The opportunity here is clear: you can stay in your community, maintain your cost of living, but access high-paying jobs that were previously only available to people willing to relocate to expensive tech hubs.

Entrepreneurship Opportunities Are Everywhere

But here's where it gets really interesting: you don't have to work for someone else. The real wealth-building opportunity is in entrepreneurship powered by AI.

AI tools dramatically lower the barrier to starting a business. Things that used to require hiring multiple people or having specialized skills yourself can now be done with AI tools and one person's creativity and hustle.

Let me give you concrete examples of businesses people are building right now using AI:

AI-Powered Content Agencies. A woman started a content agency that produces blog posts, social media content, and marketing copy for small businesses. She uses AI writing tools to draft content quickly, then edits and refines it. She can serve fifteen clients by herself, generating content that would traditionally require a team of writers. She charges each client $2,000 to $5,000 per month. Do the math. She's making more than most small agencies with far lower overhead.

Custom AI Chatbot Services. A tech-savvy entrepreneur creates custom chatbots for local businesses. Restaurants, medical offices, law firms and real estate agents all need someone to answer customer questions 24/7, but they can't afford full-time staff for that. He builds AI chatbots customized to each business's needs. Charges $5,000 to $15,000 to set up, plus $500 to $2,000 per month for maintenance. He has twenty clients. You do the math.

AI-Enhanced Tutoring. A former teacher started an online tutoring service that uses AI to generate personalized practice problems, provide instant feedback, and adapt to each student's learning pace. She charges $60 per hour for tutoring sessions that are more effective than traditional tutoring because the AI handles the routine parts (generating problems, checking answers) while she focuses on explaining concepts and providing encouragement. She works with thirty students per week and makes over $90,000 per year.

AI Image Generation for Small Businesses. An artist who learned to use AI image generators now offers custom image services to small businesses. Product photos, social media graphics, marketing materials, website images. She can produce in a day what used to take a week, and charges accordingly. She's making six figures serving local businesses that previously couldn't afford professional photography and design.

AI-Powered Translation Services. A bilingual entrepreneur offers translation services using AI tools. The AI does the initial translation, she reviews and refines it for cultural context and nuance. She can handle much larger volumes than traditional translation work, charging less per word than traditional translators but making more total because of the volume she can process. She focuses on serving businesses and organizations in the Black community that need materials translated into multiple languages.

AI Consulting for Non-Profits. A consultant helps non-profit organizations implement AI tools to increase their impact. She shows them how to use AI for fundraising, donor management, program evaluation, and outreach. Non-profits often can't afford expensive consulting, but her services are affordable because AI tools allow her to deliver results quickly. She works with a dozen non-profits, charging $3,000 to $8,000 per project.

AI Training Programs. A former corporate trainer now offers training programs teaching professionals in various fields how to use AI tools relevant to their work. Teachers learning to use AI for lesson planning. Lawyers learning AI legal research tools. Marketers learning AI content creation. She charges $500 to $2,000 per person for multi-week courses, running multiple courses simultaneously online.

Notice the pattern? These entrepreneurs aren't building AI from scratch. They're not AI engineers. They're people who learned to use AI tools effectively and built businesses around that knowledge.

This is the opportunity. You don't need a computer science degree or venture capital funding. You need to understand AI tools, identify problems they can solve, and have the hustle to build a business around that.

An entrepreneur I spoke with put it this way: "AI is like electricity was in the early 1900s. You didn't need to understand how to generate electricity to build a successful business using electric power. You just needed to identify what electricity could do and build something valuable around that. AI is the same. You don't need to build the AI. You need to build valuable services using AI."

The businesses being built right now by everyday people using AI tools are going to be the established players in five years. The people starting now are getting the early mover advantage.

Why NOW Is the Critical Time

I want to be very clear about timing because this is crucial.

We are in a narrow window of opportunity right now. It's not going to last.

Think about what happened with the internet. In the mid-1990s, if you understood how to build websites, you were in high demand. Companies were desperate for anyone with those skills. You could get hired with minimal experience. You could start a web development business with basic skills. The barriers were low and the opportunities were everywhere.

By the mid-2000s, the field had matured. Competition had increased. Expectations had risen. Boot camps and degree programs were producing graduates. The easy opportunities had been claimed. You could still succeed, but it was harder.

Today? Web development is still a good career, but the early advantages are gone. The field is crowded. Expectations are high. The pay premium has shrunk because supply caught up with demand.

We're in the mid-1990s phase of AI right now. The easy opportunities are still available. The demand still outpaces supply. Companies are still desperate for people with these skills. The barriers to entry are still relatively low.

But this won't last.

Educational institutions are rapidly developing AI programs. Boot camps are launching. Certifications are being created. In three to five years, there will be a steady pipeline of people with formal AI training entering the job market.

When that happens, having AI skills will still be valuable, but it won't command the same premium. The opportunity for people without formal credentials to break into the field will narrow. The entrepreneurial opportunities will be more competitive.

A venture capitalist I spoke with said he's seeing

"an explosion of AI startups, but it's going to consolidate." Right now, there's room for hundreds of small AI-powered businesses. But as the market matures, the bigger players will dominate and squeeze out smaller competitors. The businesses that establish themselves now will have advantages that new entrants won't have.

The gold rush analogy is appropriate. During actual gold rushes, the people who got there early found gold relatively easily. As more prospectors arrived, you had to work harder and go further to find gold. Eventually, only large mining operations with significant capital could profitably extract gold.

We're in the early prospecting phase of the AI gold rush. There's still gold lying around for people who know where to look. But the window is closing.

An economist I know tracks technology adoption cycles. She said something that stuck with me: "The difference between early adopters and laggards in new technology isn't just a few years of timing. It's the difference between building wealth and scrambling to keep up. The people who adopted email early built businesses around it. The people who resisted until they had no choice just ended up using email to keep their old job. The early adopters captured the value. The laggards just avoided getting left behind."

Don't be a laggard with AI.

The Gold Rush Is Happening Now

Let me paint a picture of what's happening in the AI space right now because I don't think most people realize the scale of opportunity.

Venture capital firms invested over $200 billion in AI companies in 2024. That money isn't sitting idle. It's funding startups, scaling operations, hiring people, and creating opportunities.

Major corporations are allocating billions to AI initiatives. They're hiring aggressively. They're partnering with AI companies. They're looking for solutions to AI challenges. Small businesses are realizing they need AI help. Every local business, every non-profit, every church, every community organization is going to need help figuring out how to use AI tools. Most of them have no idea where to start.

This is the opportunity landscape. Money is flowing. Demand is high. Supply is limited.

But most people in our community aren't even looking. They're not prospecting. They're not positioning themselves.

They're not paying attention to where the gold is.

I met a young woman at a job fair who was discouraged because she couldn't find work. She had a degree in business administration but no job offers. I asked if she'd looked into AI-related roles. She said, "That's for tech people. I'm not technical."

I explained that many AI roles don't require deep technical knowledge. Prompt engineering, AI training, AI consulting, content creation with AI tools are all things she could learn. She was skeptical but agreed to try.

Three months later, she messaged me. She'd taught herself prompt engineering, built a portfolio of examples, and landed a remote job as a prompt engineer for a marketing company. Starting salary: $75,000. More than she would have made in most traditional entry-level business roles.

She was shocked at how accessible it was once she actually tried. "I thought AI was this complicated thing I could never understand," she said. "But it's not that hard if you're willing to learn. I just wish I'd started sooner."

That's the refrain I keep hearing from people who've successfully transitioned into AI-related work: "I wish I'd started sooner."

Don't be the person saying that two years from now.

You Don't Need Permission

Here's what I want you to understand: you don't need anyone's permission to start learning AI skills. You don't need to wait for a formal program. You don't need to get accepted into some exclusive training. You don't need a scholarship or a grant.

You can start today. For free. From your phone if necessary.

There are free courses online teaching AI concepts, prompt engineering, how to use AI tools, and more. YouTube has thousands of tutorials. AI companies often provide free access to their tools for learning purposes. Online communities share knowledge and help beginners.

A man I know learned prompt engineering entirely from free YouTube videos and practice. It took him about three months of spending an hour or two per day learning and experimenting. Then he started freelancing, offering prompt engineering services on Upwork. Within six months, he was making more from freelancing than he had at his previous job.

Zero dollars spent on education. Just time and effort.

Now, I'm not saying formal education isn't valuable. If you can access quality AI training programs, they can accelerate your learning and provide credibility. But don't let the lack of formal training stop you from starting.

The AI field is still new enough that demonstrated skills matter more than credentials. If you can show you know how to use AI tools effectively, companies will hire you. If you can deliver results for clients, they'll pay you. The formal credentialing system hasn't caught up yet, which means this is a rare moment when hustle and self-directed learning can get you in the door.

But that window is closing. As the field matures, credentials will matter more. Formal education will become more important. The self-taught path will become harder.

Right now, though? If you have skills and can prove it, you can get opportunities.

Position Yourself While the Doors Are Still Open

So what does "positioning yourself" actually mean?

It means:

Start learning. Pick one AI tool or skill area and learn it deeply. ChatGPT, Claude, Midjourney, whatever interests you. Become genuinely skilled at using it.

Build a portfolio. Document what you can do. Create examples. Show your work. Build projects. Having concrete examples of AI work you've done is more valuable than any certificate.

Network in AI spaces. Join online communities, attend virtual meetups, follow AI practitioners on social media. These networks are how opportunities get shared.

Start doing AI work. Even if it's just for practice or for free initially. Build up experience. Every project makes you more qualified for the next one.

Tell people you do AI work. Update your resume, your LinkedIn, your social media. Let your network know you're developing these skills. Opportunities often come from people who know you're available and capable.

Look for adjacent opportunities. You might not be qualified for a senior AI engineer role, but could you do AI training? Could you help a local business implement AI tools? Could you teach others what you're learning? Start where you can start.

Stay current. AI moves fast. What's cutting-edge today is old news in six months. Keep learning. Keep practicing. Keep evolving your skills.

A woman I know started by just learning how to use ChatGPT effectively for her own work. She shared tips with colleagues. People started asking for help. She offered to do small projects. That led to paid consulting. Within a year, she had a side business teaching professionals how to use AI tools, making an extra $30,000 per year. She never set out to build an AI business. She just started learning and opportunities emerged.

That's how it works. You don't need a perfect plan. You need to start moving in the right direction and adjust as opportunities appear.

The Opportunities Won't Wait for You

I want to close this chapter with a hard truth: the opportunities described here won't wait for you to get comfortable with the idea of learning something new. They won't wait for you to finish other obligations. They won't wait for the "perfect time" to start.

Every month you wait is a month someone else is getting ahead. Every month the field becomes more competitive. Every month the easy opportunities get claimed.

I'm not trying to create panic. I'm trying to create urgency. Because urgency is appropriate here.

A recruiter who specializes in AI hiring told me something sobering: "In 2023, I could place someone with basic AI skills into good jobs within a week. In 2024, it's taking a bit longer because there's more competition. By 2027 or 2028, I expect the market will be much more competitive. The easy wins are disappearing."

The door is open now. But doors don't stay open forever.

In the next chapter, we're going to talk about who's building AI systems and why that should concern you deeply. Because the opportunities we've discussed in this chapter are important, but they're not the full picture. The real power isn't just in using AI or working in AI. The real power is in building and controlling AI.

And right now, we're nowhere near that power.

That needs to change. And understanding why requires

understanding who's building these systems and what that means for all of us.

Let's talk about representation in AI. Or more accurately, let's talk about the lack of it.

CHAPTER SIX

WHO'S BUILDING AI?

I'm going to show you a picture that should make you angry.

Not literally a picture, but a statistical snapshot of who's building the AI systems that are transforming our world.

Are you ready?

At the major AI companies like OpenAI, Google DeepMind, Anthropic, Meta AI, and Microsoft AI, Black people make up less than 3% of the workforce. In leadership positions and research roles, it's often less than 1%.

At AI startups receiving venture capital funding, Black founders account for less than 1% of funding recipients.

In AI research published at top conferences, Black researchers are authors on less than 2% of papers.

In university AI and machine learning programs, Black students make up about 3% to 5% of graduate students.

These numbers should make you furious. Because AI is being built, right now, by a group of people that looks almost nothing like us. And when the people building technology don't look like the people using it, bad things happen.

Let me be very clear about what I'm saying: I'm not suggesting that white or Asian engineers are intentionally trying to harm Black communities. Most of them aren't. But intention doesn't matter when the outcome is that AI systems perpetuate and amplify existing inequalities.

You don't need malicious intent to create biased systems. You just need homogeneous teams who don't see problems that don't affect them. You need decision-makers who've never experienced the issues that marginalized communities face. You need builders who assume their experience is universal.

That's what we have now. And it's creating AI systems that work better for some people than others. AI systems that see some faces but not others. AI systems that understand some voices but not others. AI systems that serve some communities while harming others.

This isn't abstract. This has real consequences. And those consequences are falling disproportionately on us.

So let's talk about who's building AI and why that matters.

The Silicon Valley Reality

Silicon Valley likes to sell itself as a meritocracy. The best ideas win. Talent rises to the top. Anyone with skills and determination can make it.

That's the myth.

The reality is that Silicon Valley is one of the least diverse professional environments in America.

Let me give you the numbers from major tech companies' own diversity reports:

Google's AI division: About 2.4% Black employees. Leadership is overwhelmingly white and Asian male.

Meta's AI Research: Less than 2% Black researchers. The leadership team photos look like a computer science department from an elite university; which is basically what it is.

Microsoft AI: Around 3% Black employees in technical roles. Slightly better than some peers, but still far from representative.

OpenAI: Doesn't publicly release detailed diversity statistics, but based on public profiles of their research team, Black representation appears to be in the low single digits.

Anthropic: Similar story. Founding team and early hires were drawn almost entirely from elite tech companies and universities with well-documented diversity problems.

NVIDIA, Intel, AMD (the companies making the chips that power AI): All report Black technical workforce percentages in the low single digits.

These aren't outliers. This is the pattern across the entire AI industry.

Now, some people will look at these numbers and say, "Well, Asian workers are well-represented in tech. So it's not really a diversity problem, it's just about Black representation specifically."

That's a misleading framing. First, "Asian" is not a monolithic category. Indian and Chinese workers are well-represented, but Southeast Asian, Pacific Islander, and other Asian subgroups are not. Second, even where Asian workers are well-represented in technical roles, they're often underrepresented in leadership positions. Third, and most importantly for this book's purpose: the lack of Black representation is a crisis that needs to be addressed regardless of how other groups are represented.

A Black AI researcher I spoke with, one of the very few working at a major tech company, told me about his experience. "I've been in meetings where I'm the only Black person in a room of sixty engineers making decisions about products that will be used by millions of Black people. And nobody thinks that's a problem. Nobody thinks, 'Maybe we should have more perspectives in this room.' They just assume the people in the room are sufficient to represent everyone." That assumption is the problem.

It Gets Worse at the Top

The diversity numbers I just gave you? Those are for overall workforce. When you look at leadership positions, decision-making roles, and senior research positions, the numbers get even worse.

CEOs and founders of major AI companies: overwhelmingly white men. Some Asian men. Virtually no Black founders or CEOs of significant AI companies.

Boards of directors: same story. The people governing these companies, setting strategy, and making major decisions look almost nothing like America, let alone like the global population that will be affected by their products.

Research leadership: the people deciding what AI research gets pursued, what problems get prioritized, what counts as success are also mostly white and Asian men.

Venture capital partners funding AI startups: over 90% white, with less than 1% Black. This matters because VCs don't just provide money. They provide guidance, connections, credibility, and access to resources. The people holding the money determine which ideas get funded and which founders get opportunities.

I talked to a Black entrepreneur who pitched his AI startup to over thirty venture capital firms. He had a strong technical background, a clear business model, early customer traction, and a product that addressed a real need in underserved communities. He couldn't get funded.

"The feedback I kept getting was that VCs 'couldn't see the market' or 'weren't sure about the opportunity,'" he told me. "But what they really meant was that they didn't understand the communities I was serving because they'd never been part of those communities. They couldn't see the opportunity because they'd never experienced the problems."

Meanwhile, his white peers with weaker credentials and less traction were getting funded because VCs "understood" their markets, which were typically just variations of products that already existed, aimed at demographics that VCs were familiar with.

Eventually, he got acquired by a larger company for far less than his company was worth because he was running out of runway. His idea was good enough that a major tech company wanted it, but he couldn't get the funding to build it independently because of who controlled access to capital.

That story is not unique. It's the pattern.

The Pipeline Myth

When you point out the lack of diversity in tech, you often hear about "the pipeline problem."

The argument goes like this: tech companies would love to hire more Black engineers and researchers, but there just aren't enough qualified candidates. The problem isn't discrimination in hiring; it's that the pipeline of qualified Black candidates is too small. Fix education. Get more Black students into computer science programs. Then the diversity will naturally follow.

It sounds reasonable. It's also largely bullshit.

Don't get me wrong, we do need more Black students in computer science and AI programs. That's absolutely true. But the "pipeline problem" framing suggests that companies are doing everything right and just waiting for qualified Black candidates to appear. That's not what's happening.

Let me show you why the pipeline explanation doesn't hold up:

First, the numbers don't match. Black students earn about 7% of computer science bachelor's degrees. That's not great, but it's significantly higher than the 2-3% representation in tech companies. Even if you only hired from the existing pipeline, you should have higher representation than you do. The math doesn't work.

Second, tech companies overwhelmingly hire from elite universities. Google, Meta, OpenAI, and others recruit heavily from Stanford, MIT, Carnegie Mellon, UC Berkeley, and similar schools. These schools have terrible track records on Black enrollment and especially on Black enrollment in technical programs. By choosing to recruit almost exclusively from these schools, tech companies are limiting their pipeline before the pipeline problem even starts.

I talked to a talented Black programmer who went to an HBCU and got a computer science degree. His skills were solid. His projects were impressive. But he couldn't get interviews at major tech companies because they didn't recruit at his school. Meanwhile, less impressive candidates from Stanford or MIT were getting multiple offers.

"It's not that they couldn't find Black candidates," he said. "It's that they only looked in places where Black candidates were unlikely to be."

Third, Black candidates who do make it into tech companies report hostile environments and lack of support. Multiple studies have found that Black tech workers leave the industry at higher rates than other groups. It's not because they can't do the work. It's because the work environment is isolating, they face microaggressions and sometimes overt discrimination, they see no path to advancement, and they don't see people who look like them in leadership positions.

If you have a pipeline that's leaking at the exit just as fast as it's being filled at the entrance, you don't really have a pipeline. You have a revolving door.

Fourth, companies aren't actually trying that hard. If tech companies were genuinely committed to diversity, they'd recruit at HBCUs. They'd create apprenticeship programs for people without traditional credentials. They'd fund training programs. They'd examine their interview processes for bias. They'd track retention rates by race and address problems when Black employees leave at higher rates.

Some companies do some of these things. But most don't do enough of them consistently enough to make a real difference. And then they blame "the pipeline."

A tech recruiter I know said it plainly: "Companies want diversity that shows up fully qualified at their door, requiring zero additional effort or adjustment to their existing systems. They want the benefits of appearing diverse without actually doing the hard work of making their companies places where diverse employees can thrive."

The pipeline problem is real, but it's often used as an excuse for not addressing the access problem, the retention problem, the promotion problem, and the culture problem.

Why Venture Capital Doesn't Flow to Black Founders

Let's talk about money because money is power in the tech world.

Venture capital funding for AI startups is in the hundreds of billions of dollars. But less than 1% of that funding goes to Black founders.

Less. Than. One. Percent.

That means Black founders are building AI companies with scraps while white and Asian founders are building with mountains of cash. And money in tech translates directly to advantage. More money means you can hire better talent, move faster, survive mistakes, scale more aggressively, and outlast competitors.

Why is VC funding so skewed?

The official answer you'll hear is that VCs fund the

best ideas and the best teams regardless of the founder's race. They're purely focused on returns. Race doesn't matter. That's not true. Here's why:

VC funding is based on pattern matching. VCs invest in founders who remind them of previous successful founders. And previous successful tech founders have overwhelmingly been white or Asian men who went to Stanford or MIT, worked at Google or Facebook, and come from privileged backgrounds. If you don't fit that pattern, you're swimming upstream. A Black female founder I spoke with described pitching to VCs: "They kept asking me questions that seemed designed to confirm I didn't fit their mental model of what a successful founder looks like. They questioned my technical credentials even though I had a PhD in computer science. They questioned whether I understood the market even though I'd done extensive research. They questioned my ability to scale even though my initial metrics were strong. Meanwhile, white male founders with weaker credentials and worse metrics were getting funded based on 'potential' and 'vision.'"

VCs invest in their networks. Most VC deals come through personal connections and warm introductions. If you're not in the network, you're not getting the warm intro. And Black founders are systematically excluded from these networks because they didn't go to the right schools, don't live in the right neighborhoods, don't belong to the right clubs, and weren't roommates with someone who's now a successful entrepreneur. It's not (usually) conscious racism. It's structural advantage perpetuating itself.

VCs are risk-averse despite their reputation. The venture capital industry talks a big game about risk-taking and innovation, but in reality, they're remarkably conservative. They fund variations of things that have worked before. They fund founders from proven backgrounds. They fund businesses serving markets they understand.

Black founders are often pursuing opportunities in underserved markets that VCs don't understand because they've never been part of those communities. VCs see this as risky because it's unfamiliar, even when the actual business opportunity is solid.

The VC industry itself lacks diversity. Less than 3% of VC decision-makers are Black. If the people controlling the money don't look like you, they're less likely to understand your business, less likely to see the opportunity, less likely to trust your judgment, and less likely to fund you.

A study by Harvard Business School found that when the exact same business pitch was presented by a white entrepreneur versus a Black entrepreneur (using actors reading identical scripts), VCs rated the white entrepreneur as more competent and more fundable. Same pitch. Different race. Different outcome.

That's not a pipeline problem. That's a racism problem.

VCs demand social proof from Black founders that they don't demand from white founders. Black founders often need to show traction, revenue, and proof of concept before getting funded. White founders can get funded on an idea and a pitch deck. This creates a vicious cycle: Black founders can't get the money they need to build the proof of concept that would allow them to get the money.

The result of all this? AI companies are being built primarily by people with access to capital, and access to capital is heavily racialized.

When We're Not in the Room, We're on the Menu

This phrase gets used a lot in tech diversity conversations, and it's worth unpacking because it captures something crucial.

When decisions are being made about AI systems that will affect millions of people, and the people making those decisions don't include representation from the communities being affected, bad outcomes are predictable.

Let me give you concrete examples:

Facial recognition AI that doesn't recognize Black faces. For years, facial recognition systems worked significantly worse on Black faces than white faces. Studies found error rates for Black women were up to 35% higher than for white men. This wasn't because engineers maliciously programmed bias. It was because the training data used predominantly white faces, and the engineers testing the systems were predominantly not Black, so they didn't notice or prioritize the problem.

This has real consequences. Black people being misidentified by police facial recognition systems. Black people unable to use facial recognition to unlock their own phones or access services. Black people flagged as security threats due to false matches. A Black woman told me about trying to use facial recognition at an airport and being unable to get the system to recognize her face. She was pulled aside for additional screening. The experience was humiliating and stressful. "If the people building that system had included Black faces in their testing, they would have caught this problem," she said. "But we weren't in the room, so our faces weren't considered."

Healthcare AI trained on white patients. AI diagnostic tools trained primarily on data from white patients have been shown to work less effectively for Black patients. An AI system that predicts heart attack risk might miss warning signs in Black patients because it was trained on data from predominantly white patient populations where symptoms and risk factors may present differently. This literally costs lives. Black patients already experience worse health outcomes due to systemic racism in healthcare. AI that's trained on biased data makes this worse, not better.

Credit scoring algorithms that perpetuate redlining. AI systems used for credit scoring and loan approval learn from historical data. But historical lending data reflects decades of discriminatory practices. When AI learns from that data, it can perpetuate those patterns even without any explicit racial variables in the algorithm.

The result? Black applicants with similar financial profiles to white applicants getting denied loans or being offered worse terms. The AI isn't explicitly racist, but it learned racism from the data it was trained on.

Criminal justice algorithms that over-predict recidivism for Black defendants. AI systems used to predict whether defendants will commit future crimes have been shown to have significant racial disparities. They're more likely to falsely label Black defendants as high risk and white defendants as low risk.

These predictions affect bail decisions, sentencing, and parole. Lives are being destroyed because algorithms trained on biased data are making biased predictions.

Natural language processing that doesn't understand Black English. AI language systems are typically trained on "standard" English text. But African American Vernacular English (AAVE) has different grammar, vocabulary, and patterns. AI systems often perform worse when processing AAVE, treating it as "incorrect" English rather than a legitimate dialect.

This affects everything from resume screening algorithms (that might downgrade resumes with AAVE patterns) to content moderation systems (that might flag AAVE as inappropriate) to voice assistants (that struggle to understand Black voices and speech patterns).

Hiring algorithms that screen out Black candidates. AI recruiting tools that analyze resumes and predict candidate success can learn to discriminate based on patterns in historical hiring data. If a company historically hired predominantly white candidates and those candidates were marked as successful, the AI might learn to favor candidates with similar profiles; which means white candidates.

Amazon famously had to scrap an AI recruiting tool because it was systematically downgrading resumes from women. Similar problems exist for Black candidates, though they're less publicly documented.

These aren't hypothetical problems. These are

documented cases where AI systems caused real harm because the people building them didn't include diverse perspectives.

And here's what makes it worse: when these problems are discovered, the response from tech companies is often defensive. They claim the AI isn't biased, it's just reflecting reality. Or they acknowledge the problem but treat it as a technical challenge to solve rather than a fundamental issue with who's building the systems and what values they're prioritizing.

A Black AI ethics researcher told me: "Every time I raise concerns about bias in AI systems, I'm treated like I'm being political or oversensitive. But when harm happens to Black communities because of these systems, suddenly everyone wants to know why nobody caught it earlier. We caught it. We warned you. You just didn't listen because we weren't important enough to listen to."

When we're not in the room where AI is being built, our concerns aren't heard until it's too late. And by then, the biased systems are already deployed and causing harm.

The Cycle Perpetuates Itself

Here's how the lack of diversity in AI becomes self-perpetuating:

Step 1: AI companies are founded by people from homogeneous backgrounds (usually white or Asian men from elite universities).

Step 2: These founders hire people from their networks, who tend to look like them and come from similar backgrounds.

Step 3: The company culture reflects the values and

experiences of the founding team and early employees.

Step 4: When the company does try to diversify, the existing culture makes it difficult for diverse employees to fit in and thrive.

Step 5: Diverse employees leave at higher rates because the environment is unwelcoming.

Step 6: The company points to retention problems as evidence that diverse candidates "don't work out" rather than examining why the environment isn't working for them.

Step 7: The cycle continues, with the company becoming more homogeneous over time rather than more diverse.

I talked to a Black engineer who worked at a major AI company for less than a year before quitting. "Every meeting, I was the only Black person in the room. My ideas were consistently ignored or attributed to others. I had to work twice as hard to get half the credit. When I raised concerns about bias in the products we were building, I was told I was being too sensitive. It was exhausting. I left because staying was destroying my mental health."

That's the retention problem. And it's not really about whether individual Black employees can handle the technical work. It's about whether predominantly white organizations are willing to create environments where Black employees can succeed.

Most aren't. Or at least, they aren't trying hard enough.

Why This Matters Beyond Representation

Some people will read this chapter and think I'm just

asking for diversity for diversity's sake. Like it's about making sure everyone gets a trophy or ensuring politically correct representation.

That's not what this is about.

Diversity in AI development is a matter of justice, safety, and quality.

Justice: Black people will be affected by AI systems. We deserve to have a voice in how those systems are built. Taxation without representation was wrong in 1776, and it's wrong now. If AI is going to shape our lives, we have the right to shape AI.

Safety: AI systems built without diverse perspectives create real harm, as I've documented. This isn't abstract. People are being denied loans, falsely arrested, misdiagnosed, and discriminated against because of biased AI. Diverse teams catch these problems before they cause harm.

Quality: Diverse teams build better products. Multiple studies have shown that diverse teams are more innovative, catch more errors, and create solutions that work for more people. Homogeneous teams have blind spots. Diverse teams have better coverage of the problem space.

An AI product manager told me: "Every time we've added a team member from a different background, they've identified assumptions we were making that would have caused problems. We thought we were building for 'everyone,' but we were really building for people like us. Diversity isn't charity. It's competitive advantage."

So when I argue for Black representation in AI, I'm not asking for handouts or special treatment. I'm arguing for justice, for safety, and for building better AI systems that work for everyone.

What Needs to Change

The lack of Black representation in AI isn't an accident and it's not inevitable. It's the result of specific choices and systems that can be changed.

Here's what needs to happen:

AI companies need to recruit beyond elite universities. Recruit at HBCUs. Recruit at community colleges. Create apprenticeship programs. Value skills over pedigrees.

Venture capital needs to flow to Black founders. This means VCs need to actively examine their own biases, expand their networks, evaluate pitches more objectively, and take risks on founders who don't fit the typical pattern.

Companies need to create inclusive cultures where Black employees can thrive. This means examining promotion practices, addressing microaggressions, creating mentorship opportunities, and actually listening when Black employees raise concerns.

Educational institutions need to increase Black enrollment in AI programs. This means addressing barriers to access, providing support for students from underrepresented backgrounds, and creating pathways for people without traditional credentials.

The tech industry needs to value diverse perspectives. This means treating diversity as a technical requirement, not a nice-to-have. It means including diverse team members in decision-making, not just hiring them for optics.

Black communities need to push for representation. We can't wait for tech companies to voluntarily include us. We need to demand seats at the table. We need to build our own AI companies. We need to train our own AI researchers. We need to create our own funding sources if existing ones won't support us.

This last point is crucial. We can't just wait for Silicon Valley to decide we're worthy of inclusion. We need to create our own pathways.

We Need to Build Our Own

Here's the reality: we cannot afford to wait for tech companies to voluntarily become more inclusive. The pace of change is too slow. The stakes are too high.

We need to build our own AI companies. Fund our own AI startups. Train our own AI researchers. Create our own AI tools that serve our communities.

This is starting to happen. There are Black-founded AI companies. There are AI training programs specifically for underrepresented communities. There are investors beginning to fund diverse founders.

But it's not happening fast enough or at large enough scale.

I talked to a Black AI entrepreneur who's building tools specifically for underserved communities. "I got tired of waiting for big tech companies to address the needs of our communities," he said. "So I'm building solutions myself. It's harder without access to the same funding and resources, but at least I know the products we're building actually serve the people who need them."

That's the spirit we need more of. Not just asking for inclusion in existing systems, but building our own systems that serve our communities.

This doesn't mean we abandon the fight for inclusion in mainstream tech. We should absolutely continue pushing for representation at Google, Microsoft, OpenAI, and other major players. But we also need our own institutions, our own companies, our own power.

The Choice Ahead

We're at a critical juncture. AI is being built right now by people who largely don't look like us and don't understand our communities. The decisions being made today about how AI works will shape society for decades.

We have a choice: we can accept this and deal with the consequences of being excluded from AI development. Or we can fight for inclusion while simultaneously building our own AI capabilities.

I know which choice I'm making. I know which choice this book is advocating for.

The question is: what choice are you going to make?

Because here's the hard truth: complaining about lack of representation without doing anything about it accomplishes nothing. We need action.

Learn AI skills. Support Black-owned AI companies. Encourage young people in our community to pursue AI education. Demand accountability from tech companies.

Build products. Start businesses. Create opportunities.

When we're not in the room, we're on the menu. So let's get in the room. And if they won't let us in, let's build our own rooms.

In the next chapter, we're going to talk about what happens when AI systems are biased and why those biases hit our community harder than others. We're going to look at concrete examples of AI causing harm and what we can do about it. Because understanding who builds AI is just the first step. Understanding what happens when those builders don't represent us, that's what comes next.

And it's not pretty.

CHAPTER SEVEN

WHEN AI DOESN'T SEE US

In 2015, a Black software developer named Jacky Alciné noticed something disturbing about Google Photos. The app's AI-powered image recognition system had automatically tagged photos of him and his Black friend as "gorillas."

When he posted about it on Twitter, Google apologized. They said it was an error. They promised to fix it. And you know what their fix was?

They removed "gorilla" from the AI's vocabulary entirely. The system still couldn't properly identify Black faces, but at least it wouldn't call them gorillas anymore.

That was almost ten years ago. And here's what's wild: as of 2024, Google Photos still can't identify gorillas in images. They never actually fixed the underlying problem, the AI's inability to properly recognize and categorize Black faces. They just slapped a band-aid on the symptom and called it solved.

That story encapsulates everything wrong with how the tech industry handles AI bias. They treat it as a PR problem to be managed rather than a fundamental flaw to be fixed. They address the most egregious examples while leaving the underlying systems broken. And Black people continue to be harmed while they claim to be working on solutions.

This chapter is going to be uncomfortable because I'm going to show you, in detail, how AI systems fail to see us, actively discriminate against us, and perpetuate the racism that already exists in society. These aren't theoretical concerns. These are documented cases where AI has caused real harm to real people in our community.

And the worst part? This is just the beginning. As AI becomes more embedded in every aspect of society, these biases will be amplified and automated at scale.

So let's talk about how AI doesn't see us, and what that means.

Facial Recognition: The Technology That Can't See Black Faces

Facial recognition sounds like science fiction, but it's already everywhere. Your phone uses it to unlock. Airlines use it for boarding. Stores use it for security. Police use it for surveillance and identification. Border control uses it for immigration enforcement.

And it works significantly worse on Black faces than white faces.

Multiple studies have documented this. In 2018, MIT researcher Joy Buolamwini published a groundbreaking study showing that facial recognition systems from major tech companies had error rates up to 34.7% for Black women, compared to 0.8% for white men. That's a 43-times higher error rate.

Let that sink in. The technology that's being used to identify people, grant access, and even make arrests is 43 times more likely to misidentify a Black woman than a white man.

Why does this happen? Because the AI was trained on datasets that were predominantly white faces. When researchers looked at the training data used to build these systems, they found that over 75% of the faces were male and over 80% were white. The AI learned to recognize white male faces really well because that's mostly what it saw. It never properly learned to recognize Black faces because it didn't see enough of them during training.

This isn't a minor inconvenience. This causes real harm.

In law enforcement: Police departments are using facial recognition to identify suspects. When the system has a 34% error rate for Black faces, that means one in three identifications could be wrong. And who do you think bears the consequences of those errors?

In 2020, Robert Williams, a Black man in Detroit, was arrested at his home in front of his wife and daughters because facial recognition software incorrectly matched him to surveillance footage of a shoplifting suspect. He was held in custody for 30 hours before the police admitted they had the wrong person. The real suspect looked nothing like him except for being a Black man.

"The computer must have gotten it wrong," the

detective told him, as if that made it okay that he'd been arrested, fingerprinted, held overnight, and traumatized, all because of a machine that couldn't tell Black faces apart.

Robert Williams's case got media attention. But how many others didn't? How many Black people have been falsely identified, questioned, arrested, or worse because of faulty facial recognition?

In everyday life: A Black woman I spoke with told me about trying to get through airport security using facial recognition. The system couldn't identify her. She had to go through additional screening while watching white passengers breeze through. "I felt like a criminal just trying to catch a flight," she said. "And the TSA agents treated me like I was trying to game the system, when really their system just couldn't see my face."

Another person told me about repeatedly having issues with photo booth systems that couldn't detect his face properly because the lighting was calibrated for lighter skin. "I'd have to try five or six times to get it to work. Meanwhile, my white coworkers walk up and it works immediately. It's a small thing, but it's a constant reminder that you exist in a world not built for you."

In banking and security: Some banks are implementing facial recognition for account access. When these systems don't work properly for Black customers, they're denied access to their own money. Some retail stores use facial recognition for security, and false matches can lead to Black customers being wrongly accused of shoplifting or banned from stores.

The technology that's supposed to make life more

convenient is making life harder for Black people. And the companies building these systems keep saying they're working on it, keep publishing blog posts about their commitment to fairness, keep hosting diversity initiatives; but the systems stay broken.

A Black computer vision researcher told me: "The tech is there to fix this. We know how to build facial recognition that works equally well across different skin tones. But it requires intentionally collecting diverse training data, testing on diverse faces, and prioritizing fairness over speed to market. Most companies don't want to do that work. It's easier to launch with what you have and apologize when someone complains."

Hiring Algorithms: When AI Screens You Out Before Humans See You

More and more companies are using AI to screen resumes and identify promising candidates. These systems scan thousands of applications in seconds, filtering out the ones the AI thinks won't be good fits.

Sounds efficient, right?

Except the AI is learning from historical hiring data, which reflects decades of discrimination. When the AI learns that successful employees at a company have historically been white, male, went to certain schools, and lived in certain neighborhoods, it starts to favor candidates who match that pattern. Even if the algorithm never explicitly considers race, it can learn to discriminate based on proxies for race.

Let me give you a concrete example. Amazon built an

AI recruiting tool that they eventually had to scrap because it was systematically discriminating against women. The AI had learned that successful software developers at Amazon were historically male, so it started downgrading any resume that included the word "women's" (as in "women's chess club") or that came from women's colleges.

Amazon caught this one and killed the program. But how many companies are using similar systems and haven't caught the bias? Or have caught it but are using the systems anyway?

Resume screening bias works like this:

The AI might learn that "successful candidates" went to certain universities. But Black students are underrepresented at elite universities due to systemic barriers. So an AI that favors elite university credentials is indirectly discriminating by race.

The AI might learn that "successful candidates" live in certain zip codes. But residential segregation means Black candidates are more likely to live in areas the AI hasn't learned to associate with successful employees.

The AI might learn that "successful candidates" have certain types of work experience. But discrimination in hiring means Black workers have historically been excluded from certain industries and positions, so their resumes show different career paths even if they're equally or more qualified.

The AI might struggle with names. Multiple studies have shown that identical resumes with "Black-sounding" names get fewer callbacks than the exact same resume with "white-sounding" names. If an AI is trained on historical hiring data, it could learn this bias.

A Black job seeker I talked to applied to over 100 positions online, all using AI screening systems. He was highly qualified, with a strong degree and relevant experience. He got almost no responses. Then he changed his name on his resume from DeAndre to Andrew and used his middle initial instead of his first name. Same resume, same qualifications, slightly different name. Suddenly he started getting callbacks.

"The AI was screening me out before any human ever saw my application," he told me. "And there's no way to know for sure, no way to challenge it, no way to demand fairness. You just get rejected by an algorithm and never know why."

That's the insidious thing about AI discrimination. With human discrimination, at least there's someone to hold accountable. With AI discrimination, companies can hide behind the algorithm and claim they're being objective when they're really automating bias.

And it's not just resume screening. AI is being used throughout the hiring process:

- Video interview analysis where AI evaluates your facial expressions, tone of voice, and word choice. These systems have been shown to work worse for people with accents, people whose facial expressions don't match white American norms, and people whose communication style differs from corporate white culture.
- Personality assessments where AI evaluates whether you fit the company culture. But "culture fit" often means "fits the existing white culture," and Black candidates

who bring different perspectives are screened out.

- Skills assessments that may be culturally biased in their questions, assumptions, or evaluation criteria.

A tech recruiter told me: "I've seen talented Black candidates get screened out by AI systems while less qualified white candidates advance. When I've tried to override the system and push Black candidates forward, I've been told to trust the algorithm. But the algorithm is wrong. It's systematically biased. And calling it out makes you look like you're playing favorites or being political, when really you're trying to correct for the algorithm's blindness."

Predictive Policing: Automating Racial Profiling

Law enforcement agencies across the country are using AI systems to predict where crimes will occur and who is likely to commit crimes. These "predictive policing" systems analyze historical crime data and use machine learning to make predictions about future criminal activity.

The problem? Historical crime data reflects decades of racist policing practices. Over-policing of Black neighborhoods. Discriminatory arrest patterns. Racial profiling. Selective enforcement. All of that bias is baked into the data.

When you train an AI on biased historical data, you get biased predictions. The AI learns that crime happens in Black neighborhoods because that's where police have historically focused their attention. Then it predicts that future crimes will happen in Black neighborhoods, leading to more police presence, more surveillance, more stops and arrests which creates a self-fulfilling prophecy.

Here's how this plays out in practice:

Police departments use AI to decide where to deploy officers. The AI says crime is likely in certain neighborhoods, usually Black and brown neighborhoods. More police are sent there. More police presence leads to more stops, more searches, more arrests. Those arrests get fed back into the system as new crime data. The AI sees increased crime in those neighborhoods and predicts even more crime there. The cycle intensifies.

Meanwhile, similar crimes in white neighborhoods are under-policed because the AI doesn't predict crime there, so fewer police are present, so fewer arrests are made, so the AI learns that those areas are "low crime."

Same illegal activity, different enforcement patterns, and the AI amplifies the disparity.

A criminal justice reform advocate told me: "We've known for years that arrest data doesn't reflect actual crime rates. It reflects police deployment and enforcement priorities, which are racially biased. But now we're using that biased data to train AI systems and pretending the AI is objective. We've automated racial profiling and call it predictive analytics."

It gets worse with risk assessment algorithms. These AI systems predict whether defendants will commit future crimes or fail to appear in court. Judges use these predictions to make decisions about bail, sentencing, and parole.

The most famous case is the COMPAS algorithm used in criminal justice systems across the country. ProPublica analyzed the system and found that it was twice as likely to falsely label Black defendants as high risk compared to white defendants. Black defendants who didn't reoffend were labeled high risk at nearly twice the rate of white defendants who didn't reoffend.

Think about the consequences of that. A Black person with no intention of committing future crimes gets labeled "high risk" by an algorithm. Based on that label, they're denied bail and have to sit in jail awaiting trial. Or they get a harsher sentence. Or they're denied parole.

Their life is derailed by an algorithm that's wrong but that judges trust because it seems scientific and objective.

A public defender I spoke with said: "I've had judges deny bail to my clients based on these risk scores without even looking at the individual circumstances. The algorithm says they're high risk, so they stay in jail. Meanwhile, white defendants with actual criminal histories get released because the algorithm rates them low risk. The system is fundamentally broken, but because it's wrapped in the language of data and science, people trust it."

The developers of these systems say they're trying to remove human bias from the criminal justice system. They argue that algorithms are more objective than humans. But they're not removing bias. They're laundering it. They're taking biased human decisions, coding them into data, training algorithms on that data, and then treating the algorithm's output as objective truth.

It's bias with a veneer of neutrality. And it's devastating Black communities.

Healthcare AI: When the Machine Learns Medicine from White Bodies

AI is being used increasingly in healthcare to diagnose diseases, predict patient outcomes, recommend treatments, and allocate medical resources. This should be good news. AI that can spot patterns humans miss, that can process vast amounts of medical data, that can help doctors make better decisions.

But there's a massive problem: most medical AI is trained primarily on data from white patients. And bodies aren't all the same. Diseases present differently. Risk factors vary. Treatment responses differ across racial groups.

When AI learns medicine from primarily white bodies, it learns to practice medicine that works best for white patients.

Here's a documented example: A widely used algorithm for managing chronic kidney disease was trained primarily on white patients. The algorithm systematically overestimated kidney function in Black patients, making them appear healthier than they were. As a result, Black patients were delayed in getting referred for kidney transplants or receiving other critical care. They got sicker while waiting because the AI said they were fine.

This wasn't hypothetical harm. This was an algorithm used across healthcare systems affecting hundreds of thousands of Black patients. And it took years before the medical community acknowledged the problem and started implementing changes.

Another example: AI diagnostic tools for detecting skin cancer were trained primarily on images of light skin.

They're significantly less accurate at identifying melanoma and other skin cancers on dark skin. Black patients already have worse outcomes for skin cancer partly because their cancers are detected later. AI that can't recognize cancer on dark skin makes this worse.

A dermatologist I spoke with said: "I've seen AI diagnostic tools completely miss obvious melanomas on Black patients while correctly identifying less severe cases on white patients. The technology could be saving lives, but instead it's reinforcing existing disparities because nobody bothered to make sure it worked on all skin tones."

Heart disease risk prediction algorithms have been shown to work less accurately for Black patients because they were calibrated on predominantly white patient data. Black patients have different risk profiles and symptom presentations that the AI doesn't recognize.

Pain management algorithms that help doctors decide how much pain medication to prescribe can be affected by the racist myth that Black people have higher pain tolerance. If training data reflects doctors under-treating Black patients' pain (which research shows happens), the AI learns that pattern and perpetuates it.

Sepsis prediction algorithms used in hospitals to identify patients at risk of life-threatening infections have been shown to miss Black patients more often than white patients, leading to delayed treatment and worse outcomes.

The pattern is consistent across medical AI applications: systems trained primarily on white patients work better for white patients and worse for everyone else.

A Black doctor told me: "We already struggle with medical racism. Black patients having their symptoms dismissed, their pain undertreated, their conditions misdiagnosed. Now we're automating those same biases and calling it progress. AI in healthcare could save lives, but first we need to make sure it values all lives equally."

Credit Scoring: When Algorithms Become Digital Redlining

Remember redlining? The practice where banks literally drew red lines on maps around Black neighborhoods and refused to lend to anyone living in those areas, regardless of their qualifications. It was made illegal in 1968 but its effects persist today in the wealth gap, homeownership disparities, and neighborhood segregation.

Well, guess what? We've automated it.

Credit scoring algorithms and loan approval systems use AI to decide who gets loans, at what interest rates, and with what terms. These systems claim to be objective. Claiming to just analyze financial data and risk factors without considering race.

But they don't need to explicitly consider race to discriminate by race.

Here's how it works: The AI looks at zip codes, and certain zip codes get flagged as higher risk. Those zip codes are disproportionately Black because of housing segregation. The AI looks at credit history, but Black Americans are more likely to have thin or non-existent credit files due to historical exclusion from mainstream banking. The AI looks at employment history, but Black workers face discrimination in hiring and are more likely to have employment gaps.

The algorithm never says "deny this person because they're Black." It says "deny this person because of these risk factors." But those risk factors are correlated with race because of systemic racism. The effect is the same as old-school discrimination, but it's harder to challenge because it's hiding behind mathematics.

A study by UC Berkeley researchers found that Black and Latino borrowers pay higher interest rates than white borrowers with similar financial profiles. They estimated this discriminatory pricing cost Black and Latino borrowers $765 million per year. That's three-quarters of a billion dollars per year being extracted from communities of color because algorithms are perpetuating bias.

Here's a real story: A Black couple I know applied for a mortgage. Both had good jobs, stable employment history, and had saved for years for a down payment. They got denied. Meanwhile, a white couple they were friends with, with slightly worse financial profiles, got approved for a better rate. When the Black couple asked why they were denied, they got a generic letter citing "risk factors" without explaining what those risk factors were.

They suspected discrimination but couldn't prove it. How do you prove an algorithm is biased when you can't see inside the algorithm? The bank just said, "The system made the decision based on risk assessment." No human decision-maker to challenge. No clear explanation of what went wrong. Just an automated denial that felt like discrimination but came wrapped in the language of objective data analysis.

It's not just mortgages. Auto loans, credit cards, personal loans, even "buy now, pay later" services use AI credit assessment. Black applicants consistently get charged higher rates or denied outright, even when controlling for credit scores and other financial factors.

This perpetuates the racial wealth gap. When you're charged higher interest rates on everything from mortgages to car loans, you're paying tens or hundreds of thousands of dollars more over your lifetime than someone with the same financial profile who happens to be white. That's money that could have gone to building wealth, starting businesses, funding education, or supporting your community.

A financial advisor who works primarily with Black clients told me: "I see clients with solid finances get offered terrible terms on loans. They think something's wrong with their credit or their application. But often it's the algorithm making assumptions based on factors that correlate with race. And there's no transparency, no way to challenge it, no recourse. It's discrimination dressed up as data science."

The AI Feedback Loop: How Bias Compounds Over Time

Here's what makes AI bias particularly insidious: it creates feedback loops that amplify discrimination over time. Let me explain how this works:

Step 1: AI is trained on historical data that reflects existing biases (racist policing, discriminatory lending, biased hiring, etc.).

Step 2: The AI makes predictions based on those patterns, perpetuating the historical bias.

Step 3: Those predictions shape real-world outcomes (who gets arrested, who gets loans, who gets hired).

Step 4: Those outcomes become new data that feeds back into the system.

Step 5: The AI sees that its predictions were "accurate" (because they became self-fulfilling prophecies) and becomes more confident in those patterns.

Step 6: The bias intensifies with each cycle.

This is how predictive policing creates more arrests in Black neighborhoods, which creates more data showing high crime in Black neighborhoods, which leads to more predicted crime, which leads to more policing, which leads to more arrests, and so on.

This is how hiring algorithms that screen out Black candidates create workforces that remain white, which creates historical employment data showing that successful employees are white, which trains future algorithms to favor white candidates, perpetuating the cycle.

This is how credit algorithms that deny loans to Black applicants prevent wealth building in Black communities, which creates financial data showing Black applicants as higher risk, which justifies future denials, maintaining the wealth gap.

The bias doesn't stay constant; it amplifies. Each iteration makes the discrimination worse, not better.

A data scientist explained it to me this way: "If you start

with a system that's 10% biased and you create a feedback loop, that 10% bias can become 20%, then 30%, then worse, because the system is reinforcing its own biased predictions. We're not automating the status quo. We're automating an acceleration of inequality."

AI Is Learning Racism From a Racist World

Here's the fundamental problem that underlies all of these specific examples: AI learns from data, and the data reflects our society. Our society is racist. Therefore, AI learns racism.

This isn't a glitch. This isn't an unfortunate accident. This is the inevitable result of training machines on data generated by a society built on white supremacy.

Every dataset used to train AI is contaminated with bias:

- Historical hiring records reflect discriminatory hiring practices
- Criminal justice data reflects racist policing and sentencing
- Medical data reflects unequal access to healthcare and racist assumptions about Black bodies
- Financial data reflects centuries of economic discrimination
- Language data reflects both overt racism and subtle cultural bias

When you feed this data to an AI and tell it to learn patterns, it learns our racist patterns. It learns to associate Blackness with risk, with crime, with poverty, with undesirability. Not because anyone programmed it to be racist, but because that's what the data teaches.

And then we deploy these systems and act surprised when they perpetuate discrimination.

A Black AI ethics researcher told me something I'll never forget: "We keep saying we want AI to be unbiased, but that's impossible if we're training it on our world. Our world is biased. If you want AI to be fair, you have to either fundamentally change society first, or you have to actively program fairness into the system even when it contradicts what the data suggests. But most companies don't want to do that because it feels like putting a thumb on the scale. They'd rather let the AI learn from biased data and pretend that makes it objective."

The Scale of the Problem Is Only Getting Bigger

Everything I've described in this chapter? It's just the beginning.

AI is being integrated into more systems every day. Hiring, lending, healthcare, education, criminal justice, housing, insurance. Every sector is adopting AI decision-making. And in most cases, these AI systems are being deployed with minimal testing for bias, minimal oversight, and minimal accountability.

The facial recognition that doesn't work on Black faces is being installed in more locations. The hiring algorithms that screen us out are being adopted by more companies. The predictive policing systems are expanding to more cities. The healthcare AI is making more medical decisions. The credit algorithms are denying more loans.

And as AI becomes more sophisticated, the bias becomes harder to detect and harder to challenge. When a human discriminates, we can point to the decision and the decision-maker. When an algorithm discriminates, the bias is buried in millions of data points and complex mathematical operations that even the developers don't fully understand.

A civil rights lawyer told me: "I've been fighting discrimination cases for twenty years. I thought I'd seen everything. But AI discrimination is different. It's discrimination at scale, at speed, with plausible deniability. Companies hide behind the algorithm and claim they're being objective. How do you fight a system that's automating inequality faster than we can document it?"

What Happens When We Don't Act

If we do nothing about AI bias, here's what the future looks like:

Black people systematically screened out of job opportunities by hiring algorithms. Talented people unable to access careers they're qualified for because an AI learned to favor white candidates.

Black neighborhoods subjected to intense surveillance and over-policing because algorithms predict crime based on historically biased data. More arrests, more incarceration, more families torn apart.

Black patients receiving inferior healthcare because medical AI works better on white bodies. More misdiagnoses, more delayed treatments, more preventable deaths.

Black families paying more for everything including loans, credit, and insurance because algorithms perpetuate financial discrimination. The wealth gap growing larger with each AI-driven transaction.

Black students disadvantaged in education as AI systems are used for admissions, testing, and resource allocation, all while carrying forward historical biases.

This isn't dystopian speculation. This is the trajectory we're currently on.

The systems causing this harm exist right now. They're being expanded right now. The bias is compounding right now.

And if we don't intervene, the AI-driven discrimination of today will seem mild compared to what's coming.

But It Doesn't Have to Be This Way

Here's what's frustrating: the technical solutions to these problems exist.

We know how to build facial recognition that works equally well on all skin tones. We know how to audit algorithms for bias. We know how to collect diverse training data. We know how to test systems on representative populations. We know how to build in fairness constraints. We know how to create accountability mechanisms.

The problem isn't that we don't know how to fix AI bias. The problem is that fixing it isn't a priority.

Fixing bias takes time. It costs money. It might slightly reduce the performance of the AI for the majority population. It requires diverse teams that companies haven't bothered to build. It demands transparency that companies don't want to provide.

So bias persists. And we suffer the consequences.

A technologist who works on AI fairness told me: "Every time I present research on mitigating bias in AI systems, the response from companies is the same: 'That's interesting. We'll keep it in mind.' Then they launch their biased system anyway because fixing it would slow them down or cost money. They only care about fairness when there's a PR crisis or legal threat. And by then, the harm has already been done."

This Is Personal

I want to be clear about something: this isn't abstract for me, and it shouldn't be abstract for you.

Every example in this chapter represents real people whose lives were harmed. Robert Williams arrested in front of his family. Patients who got sicker because AI didn't recognize their symptoms. People denied jobs they were qualified for. Families denied mortgages they could afford. Communities over-policed because of algorithmic predictions.

This is happening to people in our families, our neighborhoods, our communities.

And it's going to keep happening unless we do something about it.

In the next chapter, we're going to talk about cultural erasure and how AI is being trained on a version of history and culture that doesn't include us or actively distorts our contributions. Because it's not enough that AI discriminates against us in the present. It's also learning a version of the world where we barely exist.

But before we move on, I need you to sit with the weight of this chapter.

AI bias isn't a technical problem to be solved by engineers. It's a social justice issue. It's civil rights for the digital age. It's the newest form of systemic racism, dressed up in the language of algorithms and data.

And we can't afford to ignore it.

Because when AI doesn't see us, we become invisible.

When AI doesn't value us, we become expendable.

When AI doesn't account for us, we get left behind.

And in a world increasingly run by AI systems, being invisible, expendable, and left behind isn't just inconvenient.

It's existential.

So we need to fight. We need to demand accountability. We need to build our own AI systems that do see us. We need to ensure our children grow up in a world where technology works for them, not against them.

Because the alternative is unacceptable.

The alternative is a future where algorithms automate inequality, enforce discrimination, and perpetuate injustice at a scale and speed we've never seen before.

That future is being built right now.

The question is: are we going to let it happen?

CHAPTER EIGHT

CULTURAL ERASURE IN THE ALGORITHM

I want you to try something. Go to any AI image generator like Midjourney, DALL-E, Stable Diffusion, or whatever you can access. Type in a simple prompt: "a successful CEO."

Look at what it generates.

Nine times out of ten, you'll get a white man in a suit. Maybe one or two images will show a white woman. If you're lucky, you might get one Asian man. But Black? Probably not unless you specifically ask for it.

Now try "a doctor." White. Try "a scientist." White. Try "a teacher." Probably white, maybe Asian. Try "a family having dinner." White family. Try "a beautiful woman." White woman. Try "a professional workplace." Room full of white people.

The AI isn't explicitly programmed to generate white faces. It's learned from millions of images on the internet that when humans say "CEO" or "doctor" or "beautiful," they usually mean white. So that's what it generates.

This is cultural erasure in real-time. The machine learning to see the world as white by default. Black people as the exception, the variation, the thing you have to specifically request rather than the natural part of the default human experience.

But it gets worse than images. Much worse.
Because AI isn't just learning to visualize a white-centered world. It's learning to write history, understand language, interpret culture, and tell stories from a white perspective. It's learning that Black voices, Black experiences, Black culture, and Black history are marginal, optional, less important, less real.

And if we don't fix this, AI will teach future generations the same lie.

This chapter is about cultural erasure. About how we're being written out of the digital future even as we exist in the present. About how AI is learning a version of the world where we barely exist or only exist in stereotypical forms. And about why this might be the most dangerous form of AI bias is because it doesn't just discriminate against us in specific decisions. It erases us from the record entirely.

When AI Doesn't Speak Our Language

Let me tell you about a conversation I had with a young woman who was using ChatGPT to help edit an essay she'd written.

She writes the way she talks; with the rhythm and grammar of African American Vernacular English (AAVE).

It's not "incorrect" English. It's a legitimate dialect with its own consistent grammar rules, rich history, and cultural significance. Linguists recognize it as a distinct language variety. But AI language models? They often treat it as broken English that needs to be fixed.

She typed in her essay and asked ChatGPT to help her improve it. The AI "corrected" her language, stripping away the cultural voice and converting everything to standard white American English. The grammar of AAVE, the habitual "be," the copula deletion, the use of "ain't," the particular verb forms, the AI marked all of it as errors and replaced it with standard English equivalents.

"It's like the AI was telling me that the way I talk is wrong," she said. "That my voice isn't legitimate. That I need to sound white to sound educated."

This is happening constantly. Language models are trained primarily on standard English text. Academic writing. News articles. Books. Wikipedia. Online forums dominated by white users. The result is AI that understands standard English beautifully but struggles with AAVE, Caribbean English, African languages, and other linguistic variations common in Black communities globally.

Here's what this looks like in practice:

Voice assistants that don't understand Black speakers as well as white speakers. A study found that voice recognition systems had significantly higher error rates for Black voices compared to white voices, particularly for speakers using

AAVE features.

A man told me he stopped using voice commands in his car because the system couldn't understand him. "I'd say something perfectly clearly, and it would give me something completely different. But my white coworkers would use the exact same system and it worked fine. After a while, you just stop trying."

Autocorrect and grammar checkers that flag AAVE as errors. This affects everything from casual text messages to professional emails to school assignments. Black students get their work marked down for "grammatical errors" that are actually features of AAVE. Black professionals have to code-switch in their writing because AI writing assistants "fix" their natural voice.

Translation tools that don't properly handle non-standard English or that lose cultural meaning in translation. When you translate AAVE phrases to other languages, the cultural context and meaning often get lost because the AI doesn't recognize them as meaningful language patterns.

Content moderation systems that flag AAVE as inappropriate or aggressive. Multiple studies have found that AI content moderation systems are more likely to flag posts written in AAVE as toxic or offensive compared to identical posts in standard English. This means Black users get their social media posts removed, their accounts suspended, and their voices silenced at higher rates.

A young man I spoke with said his Twitter account kept getting flagged for "abusive language" when he was just talking to his friends using normal slang and expressions from our community. "They weren't offensive. They were just how we talk. But the AI kept interpreting it as threatening or aggressive. Meanwhile, actual racist posts in perfect standard English were allowed to stay up."

This isn't just annoying. It's cultural violence.

When AI treats your natural way of speaking as broken, wrong, or dangerous, it's sending a message: your culture isn't legitimate. Your voice doesn't matter. You need to conform to white linguistic norms to be understood by machines.

And as AI becomes more embedded in everything from education to professional communication to social media, this pressure to abandon your cultural voice intensifies.

A sociolinguist I spoke with said: "AAVE is as grammatically complex and rule-governed as any other English dialect. The idea that it's 'incorrect' English is linguistic racism, plain and simple. But AI is being trained on corpora that reinforce that racist assumption. We're building machines that perpetuate linguistic discrimination at scale."

The Histories AI Doesn't Know

Ask ChatGPT or any other language model to tell you about the history of computing. You'll hear about Alan Turing, Bill Gates, Steve Jobs, maybe Grace Hopper if you're lucky.

Ask it about Black contributions to computing. You might get Katherine Johnson and the Hidden Figures story if you're specific. But generally? Silence. The vast history of Black innovation in technology is barely present in the AI's training data.

This is true across every field. Black contributions to science, medicine, engineering, mathematics, literature, music, art, politics, philosophy; all of it is dramatically underrepresented in the datasets used to train AI.

Here's why this matters:

When students ask AI to help with homework about "important inventors," the AI generates lists that are overwhelmingly white. Black inventors like Garrett Morgan (traffic light), Otis Boykin (pacemaker control unit), Marie Van Brittan Brown (home security system), and hundreds of others are omitted unless specifically requested.

When researchers use AI to analyze historical texts, the AI's analysis reflects whatever biases were present in the original texts, which were often written by white historians who minimized or erased Black contributions.

When journalists use AI to research background for stories, they get a version of history where Black people are marginal figures rather than central actors.

When AI is used to generate educational content, it perpetuates a whitewashed version of history.

A history teacher I know started using AI to help generate lesson materials. She quickly realized the AI knew far more about white historical figures than Black ones. "If I asked it to tell me about Benjamin Franklin, I'd get pages of detail including his inventions, his writings, his political career, his personal life. If I asked about Frederick Douglass, I'd get a basic biographical sketch and not much depth. The AI had learned more about white history because that's what dominated its training data."

This creates a vicious cycle:

AI is trained on existing historical records → Those records underrepresent Black people → AI learns that Black historical contributions are minimal → AI generates new content that continues underrepresenting Black people →That content becomes part of the data used to train future AI → The erasure intensifies.

We're not just dealing with historical bias. We're creating systems that will perpetuate that bias into the future, teaching new generations a version of history where Black contributions are footnotes rather than foundational.

An archivist who specializes in Black history told me: "We've spent decades trying to recover and document the Black history that was deliberately erased or ignored. Now AI threatens to undo that work by learning from datasets that reflect the erasure rather than the corrected record. If we're not careful, AI will teach the whitewashed version of history to billions of people, and the real story will be lost again."

Image Generators and the Default White World

Remember that experiment I suggested at the start; asking an image generator for "a CEO" or "a doctor" and getting white faces?

This isn't just about occupational stereotypes. It's about AI learning to visualize humanity as white by default.

Try asking an image generator for:

- "A person" → Usually white
- "An American" → Usually white
- "A family" → Usually white
- "Beauty" → White beauty standards
- "A leader" → White person
- "Someone trustworthy" → White person
- "A normal day" → White people doing things

You have to specifically add "Black" to your prompt to get Black faces. And even then, the results are often stereotypical or problematic.

Ask for "a Black CEO" and you might get images that feel like tokenism; overly formal, trying too hard to prove Black people can be CEOs. Ask for "a Black family" and you might get stock photo clichés. Ask for "African American culture" and you might get stereotypes including basketball, hip-hop, urban settings, rather than the full complexity and diversity of Black life.

Why does this happen?

Image generators are trained on billions of images scraped from the internet. The internet overrepresents white faces in positive, professional, and default contexts. Black faces appear more often in specific contexts including sports, entertainment, music, poverty, and crime because that's how media has historically represented us.

The AI learns these patterns. It learns that "default human" is white. It learns that Black people appear in certain contexts but not others. It learns to associate Blackness with certain stereotypes because those stereotypes are overrepresented in its training data.

A digital artist I know tried to use AI image generators for a project celebrating Black joy and everyday Black life. "I wanted images of Black families doing normal things like cooking dinner, playing in the yard, reading books, having birthday parties. But the AI kept generating either overly staged stock-photo-looking scenes or images that included stereotypical elements I didn't ask for. It was like the AI couldn't conceive of Black people just existing normally without fitting into some category."

The problem extends to how AI represents Black features:

Darker skin tones are often poorly rendered or made lighter than specified. Natural Black hair textures are often misrepresented or shown as unnatural-looking. African facial features are sometimes exaggerated into caricature. Traditional African clothing is often turned into generic "exotic" costumes.

Meanwhile, white faces are rendered with nuance, detail, and variety. The AI has learned to see and represent whiteness in its full complexity while seeing and representing Blackness through a narrow, often stereotypical lens.

This matters beyond just images:

When children use AI image generators for school projects and all the "successful" people the AI creates are white, what does that teach them?

When businesses use AI to generate marketing materials and the AI defaults to white faces, who is being marketed to and who is being erased?

When AI-generated art becomes more common and it primarily depicts white people and white cultural references, whose culture is being preserved and whose is being forgotten?

When AI is used to visualize the future and it generates white-dominated futures, who belongs in that future and who doesn't?

An educator who teaches media literacy told me: "I've started showing students how biased image generators are because I want them to understand that AI isn't neutral. It reflects the biases of its training data. But what worries me is that most people using these tools don't think critically about the bias. They just accept that the images AI generates represent reality. So the bias becomes normalized."

The Monoculture Problem

There's a concept in agriculture called monoculture, when you plant only one crop in a field. It's efficient in the short term, but it's also fragile. One disease can wipe out the entire crop because there's no diversity to provide resistance. AI training is creating a monoculture of culture, learning primarily from white, Western, English-language sources and treating that as the baseline for all human experience.

Here's what that looks like:

AI that understands American culture but not African cultures, Caribbean cultures, or even African American culture in its full complexity.

AI that knows Shakespeare and Hemingway but not Toni Morrison or James Baldwin in equivalent depth.

AI that can discuss European history in detail but gives superficial treatment to African history.

AI that understands white American holidays and

traditions but treats Black cultural practices as exotic or unusual.

AI that defaults to Western philosophical traditions and largely ignores African and African diaspora philosophical thought.

AI that knows mainstream American music but treats jazz, blues, and hip-hop, all Black-created art forms, as subcategories rather than central to American culture.

This monoculture creates AI systems that work well for white Western users but poorly for everyone else. And as AI becomes more pervasive, this cultural monoculture gets reinforced and amplified.

I talked to a Kenyan developer who works in AI. He said: "I use these supposedly 'universal' AI systems, but they barely understand my cultural context. They don't know African languages beyond basic translations. They don't understand African cultural references. They treat African contexts as exotic exceptions rather than as legitimate cultural frameworks. I'm constantly having to work around the AI's cultural ignorance, which means I'm spending extra time and effort compared to Western users who the AI was actually designed for."

A Caribbean educator told me a similar story. She was trying to use AI to help develop educational materials for her students. But the AI kept defaulting to American and British cultural references that her students didn't relate to. "I'd ask it to generate examples, and it would give me examples about American holidays, American geography, American cultural touchstones. I'd have to specifically say 'use

Caribbean examples' every single time. And even then, the examples were often superficial or stereotypical. The AI didn't really understand Caribbean culture. It just knew surface-level facts."

The monoculture problem means that AI is optimized for one cultural context and barely functional for others. And since the optimized context is white and Western, everyone else has to do extra work to make AI useful for them.

When AI Writes History Without Us

Here's a scenario that keeps me up at night:

A student in 2030 is writing a research paper about civil rights history. Instead of going to libraries or reading multiple sources, they use an AI research assistant. They ask questions, and the AI generates answers with citations.

But the AI was trained primarily on mainstream historical texts that underemphasize Black agency and overemphasize white saviors. The student's paper ends up framing the civil rights movement as something white allies gave to Black people rather than something Black people fought for and won. The student never realizes they got a distorted version of history because the AI sounded authoritative and provided citations.

This isn't hypothetical. It's already happening.

AI is being used to generate educational content, write historical summaries, answer research questions, and create training materials. And the history it's generating reflects the biases in its training data.

I'll give you real examples:

Someone asked ChatGPT to summarize the history of rock and roll. The AI's summary barely mentioned the Black origins of the genre, the blues, R&B, and gospel traditions that rock evolved from. It focused primarily on white rock stars and white-owned record labels. The Black artists who created the foundation of rock music were footnotes.

Someone asked an AI to explain the development of modern medicine. The AI generated a narrative focused almost entirely on European and American doctors and scientists, barely mentioning the medical knowledge that existed in African civilizations or the contributions of Black medical pioneers.

Someone used AI to create a timeline of "important inventions." Traffic lights were attributed to white inventors even though the modern version was invented by Garrett Morgan, a Black man. The pattern repeated across dozens of inventions with credit going to white inventors who commercialized Black innovations.

A librarian who works with researchers told me: "I'm seeing more students rely entirely on AI for research. They don't verify. They don't cross-reference. They just trust what the AI tells them. And what the AI tells them is often incomplete or biased because it's drawing from sources that were biased. We're creating a generation that will learn a whitewashed version of history because they're learning from machines that were taught by biased data."

The danger is that AI makes biased information seem authoritative. When a book or article has bias, you can identify the author and their perspective. You can evaluate their credibility. You can seek alternative viewpoints.

But when AI generates information, it feels objective and comprehensive. There's no obvious author to question. The AI has synthesized information from thousands of sources, so it must be balanced and accurate, right?

Wrong. AI can synthesize thousands of biased sources and produce a summary that reflects and amplifies the common bias. And because the AI doesn't cite its sources in detail or explain how it weighed different perspectives, users can't easily identify where the bias comes from.

We're essentially creating a machine that will teach future generations a version of history that erases or minimizes our contributions. Unless we intervene.

Language Models That Don't Know Our Stories

I asked ChatGPT to tell me about important Black writers. It gave me a decent list; Maya Angelou, James Baldwin, Toni Morrison, Ralph Ellison, Langston Hughes.

Then I asked it to write in the style of Toni Morrison. The result was... bad. It had some surface-level mimicry but none of Morrison's actual voice, her lyrical prose, her deep understanding of Black experience, her particular way of seeing and describing the world.

I asked it to explain the significance of "the dozens", a traditional African American verbal game. It gave me a clinical, detached explanation that completely missed the cultural context, the community bonding, the connection to

West African traditions, the complex social rules.

I asked it to explain Juneteenth. It gave me facts about the date and what it commemorates, but nothing about what it means culturally, how it's celebrated in different communities, the mix of joy and pain in the holiday, the ongoing struggle it represents.

The AI knows about us. It knows facts. But it doesn't know us. It doesn't understand our culture from the inside. It knows what white academics and journalists have written about Black culture, but it doesn't know Black culture as lived experience.

This manifests in multiple ways:

When you ask AI to help write something with Black cultural authenticity, it produces something that feels hollow; like it was written by an outsider trying to approximate Blackness rather than someone who lives it.

When you ask AI about Black cultural practices, you get anthropological descriptions rather than living understanding. When you ask AI to interpret Black art, music, or literature, the analysis often misses the cultural depth because the AI learned from critics who were themselves outside the culture.

When you try to use AI as a writing assistant for work that centers Black characters or experiences, the AI's suggestions often ring false because it doesn't truly understand the cultural context.

A Black novelist told me she tried using AI writing tools to help with her work. "It was useless for anything involving cultural authenticity. The AI could generate technically correct sentences, but everything it suggested felt white. The character voices were wrong. The cultural references were surface-level. The emotional truth was missing. I realized the AI had learned about Black people from books written primarily by and for white audiences. It knew how Black people are portrayed in mainstream literature, not how we actually are."

The Death of Cultural Nuance

Culture is transmitted through stories, language, shared experiences, and subtle understanding that's hard to put into words. When AI learns culture from text data rather than lived experience, it gets the facts but misses the nuance.

Let me give you an example:

The phrase "I'm tired" in Black communities can mean physical exhaustion, but it can also mean a deep existential weariness with racism, a statement about systemic oppression, a reference to generations of struggle. The meaning depends on context, tone, who's saying it, who they're saying it to.

An AI trained on text might understand the literal meaning. It might even recognize that it can have figurative meanings. But it won't understand the specific cultural weight of "I'm tired" in Black communities the way it connects to a whole history and lived experience.

Or take "Stay woke." The AI knows it's a phrase. It might even know it relates to social awareness. But does it understand the origins in AAVE, the connection to Black consciousness movements, the cultural journey from community phrase to mainstream appropriation to current usage? Does it understand what it means for Black people versus what it means when white people say it?

Or consider Black humor, the way we use humor to cope with trauma, to build community, to survive. The AI might recognize that something is a joke, but does it understand why it's funny, what cultural experience makes it resonate, how it functions socially?

Cultural nuance gets flattened in AI systems. Complex practices become simplified definitions. Rich traditions become bulleted lists. Lived experience becomes encyclopedia entries.

A cultural anthropologist who studies African diaspora traditions told me: "AI can tell you what things are, but it can't tell you what they mean. Meaning is contextual, experiential, communal. AI learns from people writing about culture, not from people living culture. And there's a huge difference."

What Happens When We're Not in the Data

Here's the existential threat: if Black voices, experiences, and perspectives aren't adequately represented in AI training data, then to AI, we essentially don't exist; or we exist only as stereotypes and fragments.

And as AI becomes more integrated into how information is stored, searched, and transmitted, being absent from AI training data means being absent from the future digital record. Think about what this means:

For cultural preservation: If AI can't properly represent our culture, language, and traditions, those things won't be preserved in the digital formats that future generations will primarily access.

For education: If AI-generated educational content doesn't include us or represents us poorly, students will learn a distorted version of history and culture.

For representation: If AI-generated media (images, text, video) defaults to white representation, we become invisible in the digital landscape.

For voice: If AI language systems don't understand our language patterns, our voices literally won't be heard by the systems mediating communication.

For history: If AI writes summaries and analyses of history based on biased sources, our contributions will be continually erased.

For opportunity: If AI systems don't understand our qualifications, our work, our potential because they were trained on data that marginalized us, we'll be excluded from opportunities even more than we are now.

An archivist I spoke with put it starkly: "Right now, if you want to find Black history, you can go to archives, libraries, museums, community records. It's there. But if AI becomes the primary way people access information, and AI doesn't know Black history or represents it poorly, that knowledge becomes functionally inaccessible to most people. We'll have preserved the physical records but lost the living connection to that history because the machines mediating access can't properly represent it."

The Urgency of Getting in the Data

We are in a critical window right now. The AI models being trained today, the datasets being assembled today, the systems being built today will shape how information is accessed and understood for decades.

If we don't ensure Black voices, experiences, and perspectives are properly represented in this generation of AI, we'll spend the next generation fighting against AI systems that have already learned to marginalize us.

This means several things need to happen:

Black writers, scholars, artists, and historians need to contribute to AI training datasets. Not just passively, where our work might be scraped from the internet, but actively, ensuring it is properly included and contextualized.

AI companies need to deliberately seek out and include Black-created content, Black perspectives, Black historical records in their training data.

We need Black people on the teams curating training data, deciding what's included and how it's represented.

We need to create our own datasets that properly represent our culture, history, and experiences, and push for their inclusion in major AI training efforts.

We need to demand transparency about what's in AI training data and advocate for more inclusive datasets.

We need to build our own AI systems trained on datasets that properly represent us.

A Black technologist who works on AI datasets told me: "The decisions being made right now about what data to include in AI training will determine what AI knows for the next twenty years. If we're not fighting to be properly represented in those datasets now, we'll be fighting against our own erasure for decades. This is the moment. This is when we need to act."

Our Stories or Their Stories

Here's the choice we face:

We can allow AI to learn culture from existing data, which dramatically underrepresents us and often misrepresents us. In that future, AI perpetuates our erasure, teaching new generations a version of the world where we're marginal, stereotypical, or absent.

Or we can fight to ensure our stories, our language, our culture, our history are properly represented in AI training data. In that future, AI becomes a tool for preserving and transmitting our culture, ensuring future generations understand our contributions and perspectives.

The first future is the default. It's what happens if we do nothing. The second future requires deliberate effort, advocacy, and action.

I think about my grandmother sometimes. She grew up in the South during Jim Crow. She has stories about resistance, survival, community, and joy in the face of oppression. Stories that contextualize our present and teach lessons about our past.

If she told those stories to an AI system to be preserved, would the AI understand them? Would it capture the cultural nuance, the emotional weight, the historical significance? Or would it reduce them to simplified narratives that lose what made them powerful?

And if she didn't tell her stories to AI, if they stayed oral history or written in journals that never get digitized, what happens when AI becomes the primary way people access history? Her stories, and millions like them, effectively disappear because they are not in the dataset.

That's what's at stake. Not just fair representation in AI systems. The preservation and transmission of our culture itself.

The Next Generation Needs to Hear Our Stories

In the next chapter, we're going to talk about what we stand to lose economically if we don't engage with AI. But I want you to understand that the stakes are higher than economics.

This is about whether our children and grandchildren will grow up in a digital world that knows who we are, values what we've contributed, and understands our humanity. Or whether they'll grow up in a digital world that's learned to see us as marginal, stereotypical, or absent entirely.

When AI doesn't see us, when our stories are missing from the algorithm, when our voices aren't in the training data, we don't just lose representation. We lose cultural continuity. We lose the ability to pass our heritage to future generations through the digital means they'll primarily use.

This isn't just about today. This is about what the future remembers about us.

And if we don't act now, the future might not remember us at all.

So we have work to do. We need to tell our stories loudly and repeatedly until AI can't help but hear them. We need to demand that our perspectives are included. We need to create datasets that properly represent us. We need to build AI systems that actually see us.

Because the alternative, being erased from the digital future, is unacceptable.

Our ancestors survived being erased from written history. They told their stories orally, passed them down, kept them alive despite systematic attempts to destroy our history and culture.

We have to do the same thing for the digital age. We have to ensure our stories survive in the datasets, in the algorithms, in the AI systems that will mediate how future generations understand the world.

Our stories matter.

Our voices matter.

Our culture matters.

And we can't let machines teach a future that doesn't include us.

In the next chapter, let's talk about money, because while cultural erasure threatens our identity, economic exclusion from AI threatens our survival.

Both matter. Both demand action. Both require us to show up and fight.

Let's keep going.

CHAPTER NINE

THE ECONOMIC COST OF SITTING OUT

Let me tell you about two people I know who both understood AI was important, but only one of them did something about it.

The first person, let's call him Marcus, was a customer service supervisor at a tech company in 2019. He saw ChatGPT when it came out in late 2022 and thought it was interesting. He read articles about AI. He talked with friends about how it might change things. He worried about his job security. But he didn't take action. He didn't learn AI skills. He didn't invest in AI companies. He didn't position himself for the changes coming.

In 2024, his company implemented an AI customer service system. His department went from forty-five people to twelve. Marcus wasn't one of the twelve. He got a severance package and has been looking for work ever since. Most companies in his field are doing the same thing his old company did, replacing human workers with AI.

He's 51 years old. He has a mortgage and two kids in college. His severance runs out in three months. He's terrified.

The second person, let's call her Jasmine, was working retail in 2020. She saw the same AI developments Marcus saw. But she made different choices. She spent evenings and weekends learning about AI. She taught herself prompt engineering. She started freelancing, offering AI-enhanced content creation services. By 2023, she was making more from her side business than from retail. She quit and went full-time. Today she runs a small AI consulting agency with five employees, making over $200,000 per year.

Same starting point. Same awareness of AI's importance. Completely different outcomes.

Marcus is losing wealth. Jasmine is building it.

This chapter is about wealth; who's building it and who's losing it in the AI revolution. And I need to be very clear: we are collectively on track to miss the largest wealth creation opportunity in modern history. Again.

The numbers are staggering. The patterns are familiar. The consequences are devastating.

And it's happening right now.

The Numbers That Should Wake You Up

Let me give you some numbers that should make you sit up and pay attention.

The AI industry is projected to be worth **$15.7 trillion** by 2030. That's trillion with a T. That's more than the entire GDP of China. That's wealth creation on a scale we've rarely seen.

For context, the Internet Revolution created an estimated $10 trillion in value over twenty years. AI is projected to create more wealth in less time.

Where is that wealth going? Who's capturing it?

Not us.

Black ownership of AI startups: less than 1%. Out of the billions being invested in AI companies, less than one penny on the dollar is going to Black founders. When those AI companies go public or get acquired, when the founders and early employees make millions or billions, we won't be among them.

Black employment in AI companies: 2-3%. When those companies hire tens of thousands of high-paying jobs, we'll get 2-3% of them if current trends continue. Everyone else will get 97-98%.

Black representation in AI venture capital: less than 3%. The people making decisions about which AI companies to fund are almost entirely white and Asian. They're capturing the investment returns while we're not even at the table.

Let me put this in perspective:

If the AI industry creates $15 trillion in value by 2030, and Black ownership remains at less than 1%, that means we'll capture less than $150 billion of that wealth. Meanwhile, other communities will capture over $15 trillion.

That's a wealth transfer away from our community of astronomical proportions. And it's not hypothetical. It's happening right now.

We've Seen This Movie Before

Does this pattern sound familiar? It should. Because we've been here before. Multiple times.

The Railroad Boom of the 1800s created vast wealth.

We laid the tracks. We didn't own the railroads. Vanderbilt, Stanford, and others became some of the richest people in American history. We stayed poor.

The Industrial Revolution created the modern American economy. We worked in the factories. We didn't own the factories. Rockefeller, Carnegie, and Morgan built dynasties. We built their wealth for wages that kept us in poverty.

The Oil Industry created immense fortunes. We worked the refineries and oil fields. The Rockefeller fortune from Standard Oil still exists in the wealth of their descendants today. Black wealth from that era? Largely gone, stolen, or never accumulated in the first place.

The Computer Revolution of the 1970s and 80s created companies like Microsoft, Apple, Intel, and others. The founders became billionaires. Early employees became millionaires. We were barely present in the industry.

The Internet Boom of the 1990s and 2000s created Amazon, Google, Facebook, eBay, PayPal, and thousands of other companies. Jeff Bezos, Larry Page, Sergey Brin, Mark Zuckerberg, and others became some of the richest people in human history. Black founders? Less than 1% of venture capital funding.

Every major wealth creation event in American history has followed the same pattern: massive value is created, and we get almost none of it. Not because we're not smart enough. Not because we're not working hard enough. But because we're systematically excluded from ownership and from early participation in these industries.

Now it's happening again with AI. And if we don't break the pattern this time, we'll be having this same conversation in twenty years, explaining to our children and grandchildren why we missed another opportunity.

A economic historian I spoke with said something that stuck with me: "Every generation has one or two wealth-creation events that determine who prospers for the next fifty years. Right now, AI is one of those events. The decisions people make today about whether to engage with AI will determine their family's economic trajectory for decades. And right now, Black Americans are making the same decision they've made during every previous wealth-creation event: to sit it out and hope for the best. That strategy has never worked. It won't work this time either."

The AI Wealth Is Being Captured Right Now

People think of wealth creation as something that happens later, after companies go public or get acquired. But that's not how it works. The real wealth is being created and captured right now, while these companies are private.

Let me explain:

When a startup raises money from venture capitalists, the founders and early employees get equity and ownership stakes in the company. If the company succeeds, that equity becomes worth millions or billions. The people who got in early capture most of the value.

By the time a company goes public, most of the wealth has already been created and distributed to founders, early employees, and early investors. Public market investors make some money, but the really massive wealth went to people who got in early.

OpenAI, the company behind ChatGPT, was founded in 2015. The founders and early employees have equity that's now worth billions. When OpenAI eventually goes public or gets acquired, those people will become incredibly wealthy. The people who join now, after OpenAI is already successful, won't capture nearly as much value.

Anthropic, the AI company that created Claude, was founded in 2021 by former OpenAI executives. It's now valued at billions. The founders and early team have equity that will make them rich when the company exits. The people who join in 2026? They'll make good salaries, but they won't get the equity windfall the early team got.

This pattern repeats across thousands of AI startups. The wealth is being captured by founders, early employees, and venture capital investors. If you're not in one of those categories, you're missing the wealth creation.

And we're almost entirely absent from all three categories.

Black AI startup founders? Less than 1% of AI startups have Black founders. That means when these companies succeed, we're not among the founders getting rich.

Black early employees at AI startups? Underrepresented at around 2-3%. When these companies hand out equity to early employees, we're getting 2-3% of it.

Black venture capital investors? Less than 3% of VC decision-makers. When AI startups generate 10x, 50x, or 100x returns for early investors, we're not capturing those returns.

A venture capitalist told me: "The real money in tech is made by founders and early investors. By the time the general public hears about a company, the wealth has mostly been captured. Right now, billions in AI wealth are being created and distributed in private markets that Black people have almost no access to. When these companies eventually become public and everyone can invest, the easy money will already be gone."

The Stock Market Gains We're Missing

Even if you're not a founder or early employee, you can still capture some wealth through the stock market. As AI companies grow and their stock prices rise, investors make money.

But here's the problem: Black Americans own dramatically less stock than white Americans. According to the Federal Reserve, about 61% of white families own stock (directly or through retirement accounts), compared to only 34% of Black families. And the Black families who do own stock own significantly less of it.

This means when AI company stocks soar, white families capture most of the gains while Black families miss out.

Microsoft's stock has nearly tripled since the company went all-in on AI in 2023. If you owned Microsoft stock, your wealth increased. Most Black families don't own Microsoft stock.

NVIDIA, which makes the computer chips that power AI, has seen its stock increase over 10x in three years. If you owned NVIDIA stock in 2021, you could have turned $10,000 into over $100,000. Most Black families weren't investing in NVIDIA.

AI-focused ETFs and index funds have massively outperformed the broader market. If you were invested in these, you captured significant gains. Most Black families weren't.

The cumulative effect is enormous. White families who were invested in the stock market have seen significant wealth increases from the AI boom. Black families, who are less likely to be invested, have missed those gains entirely.

A financial advisor who works primarily with Black clients told me: "I try to get my clients invested in the stock market, especially in growth sectors like AI. But so many of them are living paycheck to paycheck or just barely building emergency savings. They don't have the excess money to invest. Meanwhile, white families with generational wealth have been capturing all these gains. The wealth gap isn't just not narrowing, it's accelerating because of these investment returns that my clients can't access."

The Real Estate Connection

Here's something most people don't think about: AI wealth shows up in real estate prices.

When an area becomes a tech hub, when AI companies locate there, when tech workers move there, real estate prices skyrocket. If you own property in those areas, your wealth increases dramatically. If you don't, you get priced out.

San Francisco Bay Area: Home to most major AI companies. Median home prices have increased from around $800,000 in 2019 to over $1.4 million in 2024. If you owned property there, you gained $600,000 or more in equity. Most Black families don't own property in the Bay Area.

Seattle: Home to Microsoft and Amazon, both major AI players. Similar story. Property values have soared. White families who owned homes captured the gains. Black families who were priced out missed the appreciation.

Austin, Denver, Miami: Emerging tech hubs are attracting AI companies, and property values are rising rapidly. Again, homeowners, disproportionately white, capture the wealth. Renters and people priced out of homeownership, disproportionately Black, miss out.

But it's not just the tech hubs. AI wealth spreads geographically as tech workers buy second homes, investment properties, and vacation homes. They're driving up prices in mountain towns, beach communities, and exurban areas.

If you already own real estate, the AI boom might increase your wealth through property appreciation. If you don't own property, the AI boom is making it harder to ever afford property because prices are rising faster than incomes for non-tech workers.

A real estate investor told me: "I've been buying properties near tech hubs because I know that's where the money is flowing. Every time a major AI company opens an office somewhere, property values in that area go up. I've doubled my net worth in five years just by being early to these markets. But I look around, and I don't see many Black investors doing the same. We're missing out on this entire wealth-building opportunity while others are capitalizing on it."

The Equity Gap Is Accelerating

Let's talk about equity; not social equity, but ownership equity in companies.

In the tech industry, a significant portion of compensation comes as equity. When you join a startup, you get stock options. When you join a public tech company, you get restricted stock units (RSUs). If the company does well, this equity can be worth far more than your salary.

A software engineer at Google or Microsoft or Meta might have a salary of $150,000 but equity worth $200,000 per year. Over a ten-year career, that's $2 million in equity on top of $1.5 million in salary. The equity is where the real wealth is built.

But you only get equity if you work in these industries. And we're dramatically underrepresented.

Moreover, early employees at successful startups can make life-changing wealth from equity. The first 100 employees at a company that goes from zero to billion-dollar valuation can each make millions from their equity.

An early engineer at OpenAI might have equity worth $10 million to $50 million or more. The first 50 employees at Anthropic likely have equity worth millions each. Early employees at dozens of AI startups that will eventually be acquired or go public are sitting on equity that will make them wealthy.

We're almost entirely absent from these early employee positions. When the wealth gets distributed, we're not in line to receive it.

A former startup employee who made millions from equity told me: "The wealth I built from startup equity dwarfs anything I could have made from salary alone. And it happened because I took a risk joining a small company early. But I was able to take that risk because I had a financial safety net, savings, family support, and no debt. Most Black people I know don't have that safety net, so they can't take those risks. They have to take the safe corporate job with a steady paycheck. I don't blame them at all, but it means they miss out on the equity upside that builds real wealth."

The Compounding Effect of Missing Out

Wealth compounds. When you miss one wealth-creation opportunity, it doesn't just mean you miss that opportunity. It means you miss all the downstream opportunities that wealth would have created.

Let me show you what I mean:

Scenario 1: You miss the AI boom entirely.

- You don't work in AI, so no high salary or equity compensation
- You don't invest in AI stocks, so no investment gains
- You don't own real estate that appreciates due to AI, so no property wealth
- **Result:** Your wealth stays relatively flat or grows slowly

Scenario 2: You capture some AI wealth.

- You learn AI skills and get a job paying 40% more than your previous job
- You invest some of that extra income in AI stocks that triple in value
- You use the stock gains to buy property that appreciates
- **Result:** Your wealth grows exponentially

Over ten years, the difference between these scenarios isn't just the initial wealth captured. It's all the compound growth that initial wealth enables.

The person in Scenario 2 can:

- Invest more each year because they have higher income
- Take advantage of market opportunities because they have capital
- Start businesses because they have savings to fall back on
- Help their kids get educated and start their own wealth-building journey
- Build generational wealth that lasts beyond their lifetime

The person in Scenario 1 can't do any of that. They're stuck in the same economic position, watching others pull further ahead.

This is what's happening to our community right now. Every year we miss out on the AI wealth creation, we fall further behind. Not just by the amount we missed this year, but by all the compound growth that wealth would have generated.

An economist explained it to me this way: "The wealth gap isn't growing linearly. It's growing exponentially. When one group captures new wealth and another group doesn't, the gap doesn't just widen by the amount of new wealth. It widens by the amount of new wealth plus all the returns that wealth generates plus all the opportunities that wealth enables. That's why wealth inequality accelerates over time rather than staying constant."

What $15 Trillion Looks Like

I want to make sure you understand the scale of what we're talking about.

$15 trillion is the projected value of the AI industry by 2030. That's not theoretical money. That's real wealth that will exist in the form of company valuations, stock prices, salaries, equity compensation, investment returns, and property appreciation.

To put it in perspective:, **$15 trillion is:**

- About 15,000 times more than the entire annual budget of historically Black colleges and universities
- About 60% of the current total wealth of all Black Americans combined
- More than the entire GDP of every country except the United States and China
- Enough to give every Black American over $300,000 if distributed evenly (it won't be)

That wealth is being created and will be captured by someone. The question is: will we capture any meaningful portion of it?

At current trajectories, we'll capture less than 1%. That means other communities will capture over $14.85 trillion, and we'll get less than $150 billion.

Even a 5% share would be $750 billion. That would be transformative for Black wealth building. That could fund businesses, buy property, invest in education, build institutions, and create generational wealth for our community.

Even a 10% share would be $1.5 trillion. That would be enough to fundamentally change the economic trajectory of Black America.

But at less than 1%? We're being left behind again. And the wealth gap, which is already obscene, will grow even wider.

A community wealth advocate told me: "People don't understand the scale of what we're missing. They think, 'Oh, I'm not in tech, so the AI boom doesn't affect me.' But it affects everyone. This wealth is being created from the collective productivity of our economy. But it's being captured by a small group of mostly white and Asian investors, founders, and employees. Everyone else is generating the value through their labor and consumption, but not capturing the returns. That's extraction. That's how wealth concentration happens."

The Jobs-to-Wealth Pipeline Is Broken

Historically, good jobs were a pathway to middle-class stability and modest wealth building. You got a decent job, saved some money, bought a house, built some equity, retired with a pension.

That pathway is broken in the AI economy for several reasons:

First, the good jobs require AI skills we largely don't have. The high-paying positions in AI companies go to people with technical skills. We're underrepresented in those skill sets, so we're underrepresented in those jobs.

Second, even good non-AI jobs are being automated. The middle-class jobs that were pathways to stability are being eliminated or degraded by AI. What's left often pays less and has less security.

Third, the new wealth is being captured through equity, not salaries. Even if you get a decent job, you're not building wealth the way early employees at successful startups are building wealth through equity.

Fourth, wages aren't keeping up with AI-driven productivity gains. Companies are using AI to dramatically increase productivity, but those gains are flowing to shareholders and executives, not to workers. Workers' wages stay flat while AI-enhanced productivity generates enormous profits that go elsewhere.

The result is a bifurcated economy: a small group of people with AI skills, equity stakes, and investment portfolios building tremendous wealth, and everyone else treading water or falling behind.

We're overwhelmingly in the second category.

A labor economist told me: "The American middle class was built on a deal: work hard at a good job, and you'll be able to afford a decent life and build some wealth. AI is breaking that deal. Companies are capturing the productivity gains from AI while eliminating or degrading the jobs. We're headed toward an economy where a small tech elite captures most of the wealth and everyone else struggles. And Black workers, who were already disadvantaged, are getting hit hardest."

The Retirement Crisis That's Coming

Let me tell you about a retirement crisis that's brewing and that nobody's talking about.

Retirement wealth for most Americans comes from three sources: Social Security, home equity, and retirement savings (401k, IRA, pensions).

Social Security is based on your lifetime earnings. If AI displaces you from good jobs into worse jobs, your Social Security benefits will be lower.

Home equity requires owning a home. If AI wealth is driving up property prices faster than your income grows, you can't buy a home, so you can't build home equity.

Retirement savings require excess income to invest. If your job is automated or your wages are stagnant, you don't have excess income to save.

All three pillars of retirement security are being undermined by AI for people who aren't capturing AI wealth. Meanwhile, people who are capturing AI wealth are building retirement security at an unprecedented rate. Their high incomes allow massive retirement contributions. Their equity compensation becomes retirement wealth. Their real estate investments appreciate.

The result? A generation from now, we're going to have a massive retirement wealth gap. White Americans who captured AI wealth will retire comfortably. Black Americans who missed out will work longer, retire with less, and struggle financially in old age.

A retirement planning specialist told me: "I'm already seeing the early signs of this. My white clients in tech are on track to retire at 50 or 55 with multiple millions in assets. My Black clients in traditional industries are hoping to retire at 70 with barely enough to survive. The AI boom is creating two completely different retirement realities, and it breaks my heart to watch."

What About Our Children?

The wealth we build (or don't build) determines our children's opportunities.

Children of wealthy parents:

- Get better education
- Graduate without student debt
- Get help buying their first homeCan take career risks because they have family financial support
- Inherit wealth that gives them a head start

Children of parents who missed wealth-building opportunities:

- Get whatever education they can afford or go into debt for
- Start their careers in debt
- Can't afford to buy homes
- Can't take career risks because they have no safety net
- Inherit nothing or inherit debt

Every generation that misses a wealth-building opportunity makes it harder for the next generation to succeed.

If we miss the AI wealth boom, our children will start adulthood at a massive disadvantage compared to children whose parents captured AI wealth. And their children will face an even bigger gap.

This is how generational wealth gaps become permanent. One generation misses an opportunity, and three generations later, the descendants of that generation are still trying to catch up.

A parent I spoke with put it bluntly: "I want my kids to have opportunities I didn't have. But if I can't build any wealth, how do I give them those opportunities? My white coworker who got stock options at a tech company is setting up his kids with college funds, down payments for houses, seed money for businesses. What am I setting my kids up with? The same struggle I had. That's not good enough. We have to do better."

The Greatest Wealth Transfer of Our Lifetime

I've used this phrase before, but I want to hammer it home: **we are living through the greatest wealth transfer of our generation.**

Wealth is being created at an unprecedented rate through AI. That wealth is being transferred from:

- Workers to shareholders
- Employees to equity holders
- Traditional industries to tech industries
- People without AI skills to people with AI skills
- Late adopters to early adopters

- Public markets to private markets
- Regular people to founders and investors

And at every stage of that transfer, we're on the losing side.

We're the workers whose productivity gains go to shareholders. We're the employees without equity. We're in the traditional industries being disrupted. We're the people without AI skills. We're the late adopters. We're shut out of private markets. We're the regular people watching founders get rich.

This wealth transfer is happening right now. Not in ten years. Not in twenty years. Today. While you're reading this sentence, equity is being distributed at AI startups. While you're at work, stock prices are rising. While you're sleeping, property values are increasing in AI hubs.

The wealth is flowing. We're just not capturing it.

And every day we wait, the harder it becomes to catch up.

An investor who made significant money in tech booms told me: "Every major wealth transfer has a window. Early in the window, anyone paying attention can capture some value. As the window closes, you need more resources, more connections, more sophistication to get in. Right now, the AI wealth transfer window is open but closing. Five years from now, maybe even two years from now, it'll be much harder for everyday people to capture value. This is the moment. This is the opportunity. And I'm watching Black America sleep through it, just like they've slept through every previous opportunity."

The Hard Truth

Let me be brutally honest: if we don't change course, if we don't start capturing AI wealth, we're going to look back on this era with profound regret.

In 2040 or 2050, when the AI wealth has been distributed and the economic gaps have widened even further, our children and grandchildren will ask us: "What did you do during the AI revolution? Why didn't you act? Why did you let this happen again?"

And what will we tell them?

That we were too busy? That we didn't think it was for us? That we were scared to try something new? That we waited for someone else to solve it? That we didn't realize how important it was?

None of those answers will be good enough.

Because the information is available. The opportunities exist. The tools are accessible. The path forward is clear.
The only question is whether we'll take it.

In the next chapter, we're going to talk about the social and political costs of missing the AI boom, because wealth isn't just about money. It's about power, voice, representation, and control over our own destiny.

But before we get there, I need you to really sit with the economic reality I've laid out in this chapter.

$15 trillion in wealth creation. Less than 1% of it coming to our community. Jobs being automated. Investment gains being missed. Real estate appreciation happening without us. Equity being distributed to others. The wealth gap accelerating. Our children inheriting disadvantage.

This is the economic cost of sitting out the AI revolution.

Can we afford it?

No.

Will we accept it?

That's up to us.

The wealth is being created. The question is: will we capture any of it?

The answer needs to be yes. And that answer needs to drive action.

Because talking about it isn't enough. Understanding it isn't enough. Agreeing with it isn't enough.

We need to act.

Learn AI skills. Invest in AI companies. Start AI businesses. Position yourself and your family to capture some of this wealth.

The window is open.

But it won't stay open forever.

Let's move.

CHAPTER TEN

THE SOCIAL COST OF INACTION

Money matters. The economic cost of missing the AI revolution is staggering, as we discussed in the last chapter. But there's something even more fundamental at stake: power.

The ability to shape the systems that govern our lives. The ability to have our voices heard. The ability to protect our communities. The ability to determine our own futures rather than having others determine them for us.

This is what we stand to lose if we sit out the AI revolution. Not just wealth, but agency. Not just opportunity, but control. Not just representation, but the very ability to advocate for ourselves in a world where AI systems are making decisions about our lives.

Let me be very clear about what I mean by power: I'm talking about the ability to influence the systems and institutions that affect our daily existence. Who gets elected. What laws get passed. Who gets arrested and who goes free. What our children learn. What healthcare we receive. Whose voices get amplified and whose get silenced.

AI is rapidly becoming embedded in all of these systems. And whoever controls the AI controls the outcomes. Right now, we don't control the AI. Which means we don't control the outcomes. Which means we're being acted upon rather than acting. We're subjects rather than agents. We're being governed rather than governing.

And if we don't change that, the consequences will be catastrophic for our community.

Let me show you exactly what's at stake.

Political Power: When Algorithms Decide Democracy

Politics is fundamentally about power; who has it, who doesn't, and how it's used. AI is changing how political power is gained, maintained, and exercised. And those changes are not in our favor.

Gerrymandering has been automated and perfected by AI. Political parties use sophisticated algorithms to analyze demographic data, voting patterns, and geographic information to draw district lines that maximize their advantage. These AI systems can create district maps that pack opposition voters into a few districts or spread them thin across many districts, effectively diluting their voting power. Guess whose voting power gets diluted? Communities of color. AI-powered gerrymandering can identify and isolate Black voters with surgical precision, ensuring our votes count for as little as possible.

A voting rights attorney told me: "Old-school gerrymandering was bad, but it was limited by human ability to analyze data. AI-powered gerrymandering is devastatingly effective. These algorithms can run millions of scenarios and find the optimal map to minimize Black political power. And because it's done by algorithm, politicians can claim it's neutral and objective. It's not. It's precision voter suppression."

Voter targeting and suppression is being enhanced by AI. Political campaigns use AI to identify likely voters, predict their voting behavior, and target them with specific messages. But they can also use AI to identify voters they want to discourage from voting.

Black voters might be targeted with misinformation about voting dates, locations, or requirements. We might be bombarded with demoralizing messages designed to suppress turnout. We might be micro-targeted with divisive content meant to reduce enthusiasm or create conflict within our community. And it's all automated, personalized, and scaled through AI.

AI-generated content is flooding political discourse. Deepfakes, AI-written propaganda, and synthetic social media profiles spreading misinformation can all be used to manipulate elections and political outcomes. Black candidates can be targeted with AI-generated fake scandals. Black voters can be fed AI-generated misinformation that's perfectly tailored to exploit our concerns and fears.

A political consultant told me about an election where AI-generated robocalls, designed to sound like a Black community leader, spread false information about a Black candidate. "The calls sounded authentic. They referenced real community issues. But the information was completely false. And by the time we caught it and tried to correct it, the damage was done. That's the power of AI in politics, it can spread lies at scale with a veneer of authenticity."

Policy decisions are being influenced by AI analysis. Governments use AI to analyze data and recommend policies. But if that AI was trained on biased data, it will recommend biased policies. If the AI doesn't understand the needs of Black communities because we're not in the data or our perspectives aren't represented, the policies it recommends won't serve us. AI might recommend cutting funding to social programs that disproportionately serve Black communities because the algorithm calculates they're "inefficient." AI might recommend policing policies that target Black neighborhoods. AI might recommend housing policies that perpetuate segregation.

And because these recommendations come from data analysis, they'll be presented as objective and evidence-based, even when they're actually perpetuating systemic racism.

Resource allocation is being determined by algorithms. Which neighborhoods get infrastructure improvements? Where do new schools get built? How is public health funding distributed? Increasingly, these decisions are being made with the help of AI systems analyzing data about need and impact.

But if the data underrepresents our communities or misrepresents our needs, the resources won't flow to us. The algorithm will systematically direct resources away from Black neighborhoods while claiming to be neutral and data-driven.

The result? Our political power is being undermined by AI systems we don't control, using methods we can't easily challenge, producing outcomes that harm us while claiming to be neutral.

If we can't influence the AI systems shaping political outcomes, we can't protect our political power. We become subjects of an algorithmic political process that we have no voice in.

Criminal Justice: Automated Injustice

I touched on this in earlier chapters, but I need to drive this point home: AI in criminal justice is creating an automated system of racial oppression that's more efficient and harder to challenge than human bias.

AI risk assessment tools are being used at every stage of the criminal justice system:

- **Pretrial:** Algorithms decide who gets released on bail and who stays in jail awaiting trial
- **Sentencing:** Algorithms provide risk scores that influence how long someone goes to prison
- **Parole:** Algorithms decide who gets parole and who stays incarcerated
- **Probation:** Algorithms monitor people and decide when they've violated probation

At every stage, these algorithms have been shown to be biased against Black defendants. We're more likely to be labeled high risk. We're more likely to be denied bail. We're more likely to get longer sentences. We're more likely to be denied parole. And when we challenge these decisions, we're told, "The algorithm says you're high risk." How do you fight an algorithm?

A man I spoke with was denied parole three times based on a risk assessment algorithm that labeled him high risk for reoffending. He'd been a model prisoner. He'd completed every program available. He had a job and housing lined up. But the algorithm said he was high risk, and that was enough for the parole board to deny him.

"Nobody could explain why the algorithm labeled me high risk," he told me after he was finally released. "They just said that's what the data showed. But I served extra years in prison because of a machine that I couldn't question, couldn't challenge, couldn't even understand. How is that justice?"

Predictive policing is concentrating police presence in Black neighborhoods based on historical crime data that reflects biased policing. The AI predicts crime where police have historically made arrests, which is where police have historically focused their attention, which is Black neighborhoods.

More police presence leads to more stops, searches, and arrests. Those arrests feed back into the system as "crime data." The AI sees increasing crime in Black neighborhoods and predicts even more crime there. Police send more officers. More arrests happen. The cycle intensifies.

Meanwhile, similar crimes in white neighborhoods go unpoliced and unreported, so the AI doesn't predict crime there, so police don't patrol there, so crimes go undetected.

The result is a self-fulfilling prophecy of racial targeting automated by AI.

Surveillance technology powered by AI is being deployed disproportionately in Black communities. Facial recognition cameras. License plate readers. Predictive analytics linking people to potential crimes. AI analysis of social media to identify "potential threats."

A young man told me the police showed up at his door because an AI system flagged him as a potential participant in a crime that hadn't even happened yet. The AI had analyzed his social media connections, his location data, and his demographic profile and decided he was a threat. He hadn't done anything. The algorithm just predicted he might.

"I'm being criminalized for who I am and who I know, not for anything I've done," he said. "And there's no way to prove the algorithm wrong because it's predicting something that hasn't happened. How do you prove you're not going to commit a crime that you weren't planning to commit in the first place?"

AI in interrogations and evidence analysis is being developed to detect deception, analyze witness statements, and evaluate evidence. But if these systems are trained on biased data, they'll be more likely to label Black suspects as deceptive and less likely to believe Black witnesses.

Body cameras with AI analysis are being deployed to automatically flag police interactions that might be problematic. Sounds good, right? Except the AI decides what counts as problematic. If it's trained to see Black people as threatening, it might flag innocent behavior as suspicious while missing actual misconduct toward Black people.

The fundamental problem is this: We're automating a criminal justice system that's already deeply racist. The AI is learning from a system built on racial oppression and replicating that oppression at scale with greater efficiency. And because it's wrapped in the language of objectivity and data, it's harder to challenge. You can protest a racist judge. How do you protest a racist algorithm that nobody fully understands and that claims to be neutral?

A public defender told me: "AI in criminal justice is creating a nightmare for my clients. They're being judged by systems they can't confront, can't cross-examine, can't challenge. The Sixth Amendment guarantees the right to confront your accusers, but how do you confront an algorithm? The system is denying due process while claiming to be more fair than human judgment. It's Kafka meets Jim Crow."

Education: When AI Teaches Our Children

AI is being integrated into education at every level. AI tutors. AI grading. AI curriculum design. AI college admissions. And almost none of it was designed with Black children in mind.

AI tutoring systems are being positioned as a solution to educational inequality. They can provide personalized instruction at scale, adapting to each student's learning pace and style.

Except they don't understand Black children.

They don't understand AAVE, so they might mark Black children as having comprehension problems when really it's a linguistic difference.

They don't understand Black cultural references, so they can't connect learning to Black students' lived experiences.

They don't understand the specific challenges Black

students face, so they can't provide appropriate support.

They're trained primarily on data from white students, so they're optimized for white learning patterns.

A Black teacher told me about watching her students struggle with an AI tutoring system. "The AI couldn't understand how my students communicated. It kept asking them to rephrase things. It couldn't connect the material to their cultural context. It kept giving examples that were irrelevant to their lives. My students were smart, but the AI made them feel dumb because it wasn't designed for them."

AI grading and assessment is being used to evaluate student work, from essays to math problems. But if the AI was trained on standard white English and conventional white cultural references, it might downgrade Black students' work that's perfectly good but expressed differently.

A student told me she got a lower grade from an AI essay grader than her teacher gave her. "The AI said my writing was 'unclear' and 'lacked academic tone.' But my teacher said it was excellent, just in my own voice. The AI wanted me to sound white. My teacher appreciated my authentic voice."

College admissions are using AI to evaluate applications. These systems analyze essays, activities, recommendations, and other factors to predict student success. But if they're trained on historical data that reflects bias in admissions and outcomes, they'll perpetuate that bias. Black students might be downgraded for attending under-resourced schools. For having "non-traditional" activities that the AI doesn't recognize as valuable. For writing about racial experiences that the AI doesn't know how to evaluate. For having recommendations from teachers at schools the AI hasn't learned to trust.

Curriculum is being designed with AI assistance. AI systems analyze educational standards and learning outcomes to recommend what should be taught and how. But if the AI doesn't understand the importance of Black history, Black contributions, and Black perspectives, those things won't be adequately represented in AI-designed curriculum.

We're already fighting to keep Black history in schools against political efforts to remove it. AI curriculum design that doesn't prioritize Black history will make that fight harder.

Tracking and placement decisions are being made with AI assistance. Which students get placed in advanced classes? Who gets recommended for gifted programs? Who gets flagged for special education?

If the AI is making these decisions based on biased historical patterns, Black students will continue to be underrepresented in advanced programs and overrepresented in special education placements.

The result? An educational system where AI is making decisions about our children's learning, assessment, advancement, and opportunities, decisions based on systems that don't understand our children, weren't designed for our children, and actively disadvantage our children.

If we don't have a voice in how AI is used in education, we can't protect our children from biased systems that will limit their potential.

A parent told me: "I thought technology in education would level the playing field. Instead, I'm watching AI systems create new barriers for my kids. They're being assessed by systems that don't value their culture, taught by systems that don't connect to their experience, and judged by systems that don't understand their brilliance. And I'm told this is progress."

Healthcare: Life and Death Decisions by Algorithm

Healthcare is literally life and death. And increasingly, AI is making healthcare decisions. Who gets treatment? What treatment do they get? How urgently? At what cost?

When AI makes healthcare decisions, and that AI doesn't understand Black bodies and Black health experiences, Black people die.

Diagnostic AI is being used to analyze medical images, lab results, and symptoms to identify diseases. But if it was trained primarily on data from white patients, it will be less accurate for Black patients.

We've already discussed this, AI that can't detect skin cancer on dark skin, that misestimates kidney function in Black patients, and that doesn't recognize disease patterns that present differently in Black bodies.

But let me make this concrete: when diagnostic AI misses cancer, someone dies. When it underestimates disease severity, treatment gets delayed and someone suffers or dies. When it doesn't recognize symptoms, conditions get worse and someone's quality of life deteriorates.

This isn't theoretical. This is happening right now. Black patients are dying or suffering because AI systems don't see us properly.

Treatment recommendation AI is being used to suggest what treatments patients should receive. These systems analyze medical literature, treatment outcomes, and patient characteristics to recommend interventions.

But if the medical literature reflects historical biases (doctors taking Black pain less seriously, Black patients receiving inferior care, research conducted primarily on white patients), the AI learns those biases and perpetuates them.

An AI might recommend less aggressive pain management for Black patients. Less intensive treatment options. Shorter hospital stays. All based on patterns learned from biased historical data.

Resource allocation AI is being used to decide how to distribute limited medical resources. During COVID-19, some hospitals used AI to help decide which patients got ICU beds, ventilators, and experimental treatments.

These algorithms considered factors like age, comorbidities, and predicted survival rates. But Black patients are more likely to have comorbidities due to systemic health inequities. Using comorbidities as a factor systematically disadvantages Black patients in life-or-death resource allocation decisions.

Health insurance AI is being used to make coverage decisions. Which treatments are approved? Which are denied? How much does insurance pay?

If the AI is trained to minimize insurance costs, and if Black patients historically have poorer health outcomes (due to systemic factors, not biological differences), the AI might recommend denying treatments for Black patients who are deemed "high cost" or "low benefit."

A woman told me her insurance denied coverage for a potentially life-saving treatment. "They said the algorithm determined it wasn't medically necessary based on my risk profile. But my doctor disagreed. She said I needed it. We appealed and eventually got it approved, but it took months and tremendous stress. If I hadn't had a doctor willing to fight for me, I might have died because an algorithm decided I wasn't worth the cost."

Public health AI is being used to identify disease outbreaks, predict health trends, and allocate public health resources. If this AI doesn't adequately consider Black communities, either because we're underrepresented in the data or because our health needs are misunderstood, public health responses won't serve us.

During COVID-19, some AI models underestimated the pandemic's impact on Black communities because they didn't account for the structural factors that made us more vulnerable. Resources didn't flow where they were most needed because the AI didn't see our need.

The fundamental issue: AI is making healthcare decisions that profoundly affect whether we live or die, whether we suffer or heal, whether we get care or get denied. And we have almost no voice in how these systems are designed or deployed.

A Black doctor told me: "I went into medicine to help people. But increasingly, I'm being overruled by AI systems that don't understand my patients. The algorithm says don't admit them, but I know they need to be admitted. The algorithm denies treatment, but I know they need that treatment. I'm fighting the AI on behalf of my patients, but I'm one person and the algorithm is everywhere. We need more than individual doctors fighting individual AI decisions. We need the AI itself to be redesigned to properly serve Black patients."

Social Media: Algorithmic Silencing

Social media algorithms determine what content gets seen, what gets suppressed, and who has a voice in the digital public square. And those algorithms are systematically suppressing Black voices and Black content.

Content moderation AI disproportionately flags content from Black users. Multiple studies have found that posts written in AAVE are more likely to be flagged as "toxic" or "abusive" even when they're not. The AI misinterprets our communication style as aggressive or inappropriate.

Black activists, artists, and community voices are getting their content removed or their accounts suspended at higher rates than white users posting similar content.

A Black content creator told me: "I've had posts removed for 'violating community standards' when white creators post similar things without issue. I've had my account suspended for language that's normal in my community but that the AI flags as offensive. Meanwhile, actual racist content targeting us stays up because the AI doesn't recognize it. The algorithm is literally silencing us while amplifying our oppressors."

Recommendation algorithms determine whose content gets promoted and whose gets buried. These algorithms favor content that fits certain patterns, and those patterns are based on what has been successful historically, which is predominantly white-created content.

Black creators find that their content gets less reach, less engagement, less visibility than white creators with similar content. The algorithm decides what's "engaging" based on patterns that favor white creators and white audiences.

A Black musician told me his music gets dramatically less algorithmic promotion than white artists making similar music. "The algorithm doesn't recognize my music as valuable. It doesn't recommend it. It doesn't push it to new listeners. I have to work ten times as hard to get a fraction of the exposure that mediocre white artists get automatically because the algorithm promotes them."

Trending algorithms decide what topics and content become viral. These algorithms can suppress Black voices and Black issues even when they're being widely discussed in our community.

During periods of racial justice activism, multiple Black activists and journalists have documented that the algorithms seemed to suppress content about police violence, systemic racism, and racial justice. Posts would get limited reach. Hashtags wouldn't trend. Videos would get buried.

Meanwhile, content dismissing or opposing racial justice movements would get amplified.

Ad targeting algorithms determine who sees advertising, including political ads and commercial ads. These algorithms can be used to show different messages to different communities, or to exclude certain communities entirely.

Black users might see predatory loan ads while white users see legitimate financial services. Black neighborhoods might be excluded from ads for job opportunities or housing. Black voters might be targeted with voter suppression messages.

Search algorithms determine what information people find. If you search for "Black hair," what do you see? For years, major search engines returned results suggesting Black hair was unprofessional or needed to be "fixed." Search for "successful CEO" and the algorithm shows predominantly white faces, as we discussed earlier. The algorithm shapes what people, including us, see as normal, professional, beautiful, and successful. And it's showing us a white-centered world.

The result? Our voices are being systematically suppressed in digital spaces while content that harms us gets amplified. We're losing the ability to communicate with our community, organize for change, share our culture, and shape narratives about ourselves.

In an era where the digital public square is where discourse happens and power is exercised, algorithmic silencing is a direct assault on our political and social power.

A digital rights activist told me: "Social media algorithms are the new gatekeepers determining whose voices matter and whose don't. And just like the old gatekeepers, they're suppressing Black voices. The difference is that these gatekeepers are algorithms that claim to be neutral. But there's nothing neutral about systems that systematically silence one community while amplifying another."

Cultural Representation: Erased From the Digital Future

Beyond specific systems, there's a broader issue: our cultural representation in the digital world that AI is creating.

When AI generates images, as we've discussed, it defaults to white faces and white cultural references. If AI becomes the primary way visual content is created for media, advertising, education, and entertainment, what does it mean that the AI defaults to a white world?

It means our children will grow up in a digital landscape where AI-generated content overwhelmingly represents whiteness as normal and Blackness as exception. Where the images they see, the media they consume, the virtual worlds they inhabit are all white-centered by default.

When AI generates text, it draws from a corpus that underrepresents our voices and experiences. If AI becomes a primary way content is created, our stories will continue to be told rarely and told poorly.

Imagine AI-generated textbooks that barely mention Black history. AI-generated news that doesn't cover Black communities. AI-generated entertainment that rarely includes Black characters or tells Black stories.

When AI creates virtual worlds, who gets represented in those worlds? The metaverse, virtual reality, and AI-generated games and experiences, if these are created by AI trained on white-centered data, will be white-centered worlds.

Our children might grow up in digital worlds where they rarely see themselves, where their culture isn't represented, where their existence is marginal.

When AI curates culture, recommending music, art, literature, and film, whose culture does it promote? If the algorithm doesn't understand or value Black culture, it won't recommend it. Our cultural production will be buried while white cultural production gets amplified.

The long-term consequence: cultural erasure. Not just in historical records, as we discussed before, but in the living digital culture that future generations will inhabit.

If AI is creating and curating the digital world, and AI doesn't see us or value our culture, we become invisible. Not just to others, but potentially to ourselves and our children.

An artist told me: "I'm watching AI create a digital future that doesn't include us. The images it generates are white. The stories it tells are white. The culture it promotes is white. If this continues, what does that mean for Black art, Black stories, Black culture? Do we just disappear from the digital landscape? Does my grandchild grow up in a virtual world where people who look like her barely exist?"

The Fundamental Choice: Control or Be Controlled

Everything I've described in this chapter comes down to one fundamental question: **Will we control the technology, or will the technology control us?**

Right now, we're being controlled. AI systems are making decisions about our political power, our freedom, our children's education, our health, our voices, and our cultural survival. And we have almost no say in how those systems work.

We're not in the room where AI is designed. So it doesn't reflect our needs or values.

We're not making the decisions about how AI is deployed. So it gets used in ways that harm us.

We're not setting the policies that govern AI. So the rules favor those with power and perpetuate inequality.

We're not building the AI systems that could serve our community. So we're dependent on systems built by and for others.

If we continue on this path, we're accepting a future where algorithms written by others make decisions about every aspect of our lives. Where we have no agency, no voice, no power over the systems that govern us.

That's not just inequality. That's subjugation.

A scholar studying technology and social justice told me: "Throughout history, those who controlled the dominant technology of the era controlled society. Those who controlled agriculture controlled the feudal economy. Those who controlled factories controlled the industrial economy. Those who control digital technology control the information economy. AI is the next dominant technology. If we don't control any of it, we don't control any of our collective destiny."

This Is About Self-Determination

I want to be very clear about what's at stake here. This isn't just about being included in the tech industry. This isn't just about diversity and representation. This is about **self-determination**. The ability of our community to make decisions about our own lives and futures.

Throughout American history, we've fought for self-determination:

- The right to be free from slavery
- The right to vote
- The right to live where we choose
- The right to equal education
- The right to equal treatment under law
- The right to economic opportunity

Each of these struggles was fundamentally about self-determination; about our ability to control our own destiny rather than having others control it for us.

AI is the next frontier in that struggle.

If we don't have a voice in how AI is designed and deployed, we lose self-determination in the digital age. We become subjects of algorithmic systems we don't control, making decisions we don't influence, perpetuating outcomes we don't consent to.

That's unacceptable.

Our ancestors didn't survive slavery, Jim Crow, segregation, discrimination, and every other assault on our humanity just so we could be subjugated by algorithms.

We have to fight for self-determination in the age of AI just as fiercely as our ancestors fought for self-determination in their eras.

And that fight requires action:

We need to learn AI so we can understand and challenge the systems affecting us.

We need to build AI so we can create systems that serve our community.

We need to influence AI policy so the rules protect rather than harm us.

We need to demand accountability from AI systems making decisions about our lives.

We need to ensure our voices, experiences, and perspectives are represented in AI training data.

We need to create economic power in the AI industry so we have leverage to demand change.

We need to build institutions that can deploy AI in service of our community rather than being dependent on others.

This is the social cost of inaction: losing control over our own destiny in an AI-powered world. Accepting subjugation by algorithmic systems. Surrendering our power to shape the future. That cost is too high. We can't afford it. We won't accept it. We have to fight it.

The Intersection of Economic and Social Power

Here's what connects this chapter to the last one: economic power and social power are intertwined.

When we lack economic power in the AI industry, we

lack social power too.

Companies listen to shareholders and customers. If we're neither, they don't listen to us.

Politicians listen to donors and industries. If we're not economically represented in the AI industry, we have no political leverage over AI policy.

Cultural gatekeepers respond to market power. If we have no economic stake in AI platforms and systems, we can't influence how they represent or serve us.

Economic power creates social power. Economic powerlessness ensures social powerlessness.

That's why we can't separate the fight for economic inclusion in AI from the fight for social justice in AI systems. They're the same fight.

We need to build wealth in the AI economy not just for ourselves, but so we have the power to demand that AI systems serve our community.

We need to create Black-owned AI companies not just for profit, but so we control systems that shape Black lives.

We need to invest in AI not just for returns, but so we have leverage as shareholders to demand accountability.

Every economic gain in AI is also a gain in social and political power. Every economic loss is a loss of voice and agency.

A community organizer told me: "People sometimes ask why we should care about Black folks getting rich in tech. Isn't that just capitalism? Isn't that just individual success? No. It's community power. Every Black person who builds wealth in AI is someone who can fund organizations, influence policy, invest in our community, and demand accountability from the industry. Economic power translates to social power. We need both."

What We're Fighting For

Let me be clear about what we're fighting for, because it's not just about opposing bad AI. It's about creating good AI.

We're fighting for AI systems that:

- Enhance rather than undermine our political power
- Protect rather than criminalize our communities
- Educate rather than track our children
- Heal rather than harm us
- Amplify rather than silence our voices
- Preserve rather than erase our culture

We're fighting for the right to shape technology rather than be shaped by it.

We're fighting for self-determination in the digital age.

We're fighting for a future where our children have power and voice, not just in spite of AI but because of AI.

That future is possible. But only if we fight for it.

In the next chapter, we're going to talk about our children's future specifically, what's at stake for the next generation if we don't act now. Because everything we've discussed, the economic costs, the social costs, and the loss of power and voice, all of that compounds across generations.

If we miss this opportunity, we're not just hurting

ourselves. We're limiting our children's futures.

And that's unacceptable.

So let's talk about what our children need from us in the age of AI.

And why we can't let them down.

CHAPTER ELEVEN

OUR CHILDREN'S FUTURE

I need to tell you about a conversation I had with a 10-year-old girl that broke my heart and lit a fire in me.

Her name is Maya. Bright kid. Loves math and science. Wants to be an engineer. Her school doesn't teach anything about AI. Her parents don't know anything about AI. She asked me what AI was because she'd heard about it online.

I explained it to her in simple terms. Her eyes lit up. She asked if she could learn it. I told her yes, absolutely. There are free resources online, communities for young people learning AI, tutorials designed for kids her age.

Then she asked me a question that gutted me: "But if it's so important, why isn't anyone teaching us? Why aren't my teachers talking about it? Why don't my parents know about it?"

I didn't have a good answer for her.

Because the truth, that her community is being left behind again, that the adults in her life don't understand AI because they've been systematically excluded from tech education and opportunity, and that she's growing up at a moment when AI literacy might be as important as reading but she's not being taught it, is too heavy for a 10-year-old to carry.

But it's the truth. And it's not just her. It's millions of Black children growing up right now while the world transforms around them. Children who should be preparing for an AI-powered future but aren't. Children who should be learning skills that will determine their economic prospects but aren't. Children who should be building confidence with technology but are instead inheriting our technological insecurity.

This chapter is about them. About what we're denying our children by sitting out the AI revolution. About what they'll inherit if we don't act.

And about what we owe them.

The Opportunity Cost of Ignorance

Let me paint you two pictures of children growing up today.

Picture One: Sarah

Sarah is 8 years old. She lives in Palo Alto, California. Both her parents work in tech. They understand AI. They've been teaching Sarah about it since she was six.

Sarah has already played with AI image generators, making art for school projects. She's used ChatGPT to help her understand difficult homework concepts. She's experimented with simple coding exercises that involve AI. Her parents have shown her age-appropriate videos explaining how AI works.

By the time Sarah is 12, she'll have a basic literacy in AI

that most adults don't have. By 15, she might be building her own AI projects. By 18, when she's applying to college, she'll have years of experience with AI tools and concepts. She'll be comfortable with technology that will be ubiquitous by then. Sarah isn't exceptional. She's just being raised by parents who understand that AI literacy is part of being educated in the 21st century.

Picture Two: Jamal

Jamal is also 8 years old. He lives in a predominantly Black neighborhood. His parents work hard but don't work in tech. They've heard about AI but don't understand it and haven't thought much about it. His school doesn't teach anything about AI.

Jamal is just as smart as Sarah. Just as curious. Just as capable. But he's not being exposed to AI. He's not building familiarity with it. He's not developing the comfort and confidence with technology that Sarah is developing.

By the time Jamal is 12, he'll be years behind Sarah in AI literacy. By 15, he'll be competing against kids who've been learning AI for years while he's never touched it. By 18, when he's applying to college and jobs, he'll be at a massive disadvantage compared to kids who grew up with AI.

And Jamal still won't be exceptional. He'll just be typical of kids in our community who are being left behind.

The opportunity cost is the difference between Sarah's future and Jamal's future. Sarah is being prepared for a world where AI is everywhere. Jamal is not. That difference will compound over time, creating outcomes that look like ability gaps but are really opportunity gaps.

Sarah will get better educational opportunities because she has AI skills. Better job prospects. Better earning potential. Better life outcomes.

Not because she's smarter than Jamal. But because she had access to learning that Jamal didn't have.

That's what we're denying our children: access to the learning they need to compete in the future.

And the worst part? We're denying it to them during the critical years when they should be building foundational knowledge. Every year they fall behind is harder to make up later.

A child development expert told me: "The elementary and middle school years are when kids develop their relationship with technology. If they grow up comfortable with AI, seeing it as a tool they can use, they'll approach the future with confidence. If they grow up intimidated by technology, feeling like it's not for them, they'll carry that insecurity their whole lives. Right now, we're raising a generation of Black children who are developing technological insecurity that will limit them for decades."

AI Literacy: The New Reading and Writing

In the 1800s, literacy, the ability to read and write, was the dividing line between opportunity and exclusion. People who could read and write could access information, communicate widely, participate in civic life, and pursue economic opportunities. People who couldn't read and write were limited in every aspect of life.

Society recognized that literacy was so fundamental that it made education mandatory. We understood that every child needed to learn to read and write, regardless of their family background, because literacy was essential to functioning in society.

AI literacy is becoming the same kind of fundamental skill.

In twenty years, maybe even ten years, basic AI literacy, understanding what AI is, how to use AI tools, how to evaluate AI outputs, and how to work alongside AI systems, will be as essential as reading and writing are today.

People with AI literacy will be able to access opportunities, solve problems, create value, and participate fully in the economy. People without AI literacy will be increasingly limited in what they can do and achieve.

Right now, we're in the early stages of this transition. AI literacy isn't yet mandatory in schools. It's not yet universally recognized as essential. Which means there's a critical window where some kids are getting it and others aren't.

Guess which kids are getting it? Not ours.

Elite private schools are integrating AI education. Affluent families are ensuring their kids learn about AI. Tech-savvy parents are teaching their children.Meanwhile, our kids are getting the same education we got, an education that doesn't prepare them for an AI-powered world.

By the time society recognizes AI literacy as essential and makes it mandatory in schools, it'll be too late for the current generation of children. They'll have already fallen behind. They'll be playing catch-up their entire lives.

A teacher at a private school in a wealthy neighborhood told me what they're doing: "We're teaching AI concepts starting in third grade. By middle school, our students are comfortable using AI tools and understanding their capabilities and limitations. By high school, they're doing projects that involve AI. When these kids graduate, they'll have a level of AI literacy that will give them a massive advantage. And I look at public schools in Black neighborhoods, and they're not teaching any of this. These kids are going to be competing against each other for college spots and jobs, and it's not going to be a fair competition."

That unfair competition is being set up right now. With our children on the losing side.

And unlike previous technological gaps, this one is happening during childhood. We're not talking about adults who can make decisions about their own education. We're talking about children who are dependent on us to prepare them for the future.

If we don't prepare them, who will?

The Skills Gap Is Widening Every Day

Let me be specific about what skills our children aren't learning while other children are:

Prompt engineering and AI interaction. Kids in tech-savvy families are learning how to communicate effectively with AI systems, how to get useful outputs, how to iterate and refine prompts. This is a skill that will be valuable in almost every field.

Critical evaluation of AI outputs. Understanding when AI is being helpful versus when it's wrong or biased. Knowing how to verify AI-generated information. Recognizing the limitations of AI.

Creative use of AI tools. Using AI for writing, art, research, problem-solving, and other creative applications. Understanding AI as a tool to enhance human creativity rather than replace it.

Basic understanding of how AI works. Not necessarily the deep mathematics, but the conceptual understanding of how AI learns from data, recognizes patterns, and makes predictions.

Ethical thinking about AI. Understanding issues of bias, privacy, fairness, and the social implications of AI. Being prepared to make informed decisions about AI as citizens and professionals.

Integration of AI into workflows. Understanding how to use AI to be more productive, solve problems faster, and accomplish things that would be difficult without AI.

These aren't optional skills for the future. These are going to be baseline expectations. And our children aren't learning them.

Meanwhile, children in other communities are. Not just in America, but globally.

A software developer who grew up in India told me: "In India, even in middle-class neighborhoods, parents are making sure their kids learn about AI and coding. They see it as essential to economic opportunity. Kids are taking classes, doing tutorials, building projects. By the time they're teenagers, they have real skills. And these kids will be competing globally for opportunities against American kids who aren't learning these things. The Indian kids are going to win many of those competitions."

Our children are going to be competing globally in an AI-powered economy. They'll be competing for college admissions, jobs, contracts, opportunities against kids from around the world who are learning AI now.

If our kids don't have the skills, they don't get the opportunities. It's that simple.

A college admissions counselor told me: "I'm already seeing this in applications. Students who've done AI projects, who've taken AI classes, and who've demonstrated AI literacy, they stand out." Universities want students who are prepared for the future. Students who have no exposure to AI look increasingly behind the curve. And unfortunately, those students are disproportionately from under-resourced communities, including Black communities."

The Global Competition Our Kids Are Losing

Let me make this concrete with numbers that should alarm you.

In China, AI education is a national priority. Chinese schools are integrating AI into curriculum from primary school onward. The government has invested billions in AI education initiatives. Chinese children are growing up with AI literacy as a standard part of their education.

In India, coding and AI education is booming.

Private tutoring centers teaching AI skills are proliferating. Middle-class families see tech education as essential to their children's futures. Indian children are becoming a major force in global tech talent.

In Singapore, South Korea, Japan, similar stories. AI education is prioritized. Children are being prepared systematically for an AI-powered economy.

In wealthy American communities, private schools and well-funded public schools are providing AI education. Children from affluent families are getting access to learning that prepares them.

In our communities? Almost nothing. Our children are being left out of a global educational race.

And this matters because the economy is global. AI makes it even more global because AI tools enable remote work and global collaboration. Your child will be competing for opportunities against children from all over the world.

A child in China learning AI from age 10 will have eight years of experience by age 18. A child in our community who doesn't start learning AI until college (if they make it to college and if they study something AI-related) will be starting with zero years of experience. **That's an eight-year head start for the competition.**

How is that fair? How do we expect our children to compete?

An economist studying global workforce trends told me: "The next generation of talent is being educated globally, and AI education is becoming a differentiator. Countries that are investing in AI literacy for their children are preparing them to capture economic opportunities. Countries and communities that aren't are preparing their children to be left behind. America as a whole is falling behind in this race, but Black American communities are falling behind even faster. We're setting up a future where Black American children are at a disadvantage not just compared to white American children, but compared to children globally."

The Confidence Gap We're Creating

Beyond skills, there's something more insidious happening: we're creating a confidence gap.

When children grow up around technology, when they're encouraged to experiment with it, when they see people who look like them succeeding with it, they develop confidence. They believe they belong in tech spaces. They believe they can learn and master technological skills.

When children don't grow up around technology, when they're not encouraged to engage with it, when they never see people who look like them succeeding in tech, they develop insecurity. They believe tech isn't for them. They believe they can't learn it. They don't try because they're convinced they'll fail.

This confidence gap is more damaging than the skills gap. Skills can be learned. Confidence is harder to build.

I've met too many Black teenagers and young adults who say, "I'm not good with computers" or "Tech stuff isn't for me" or "I'm not smart enough for that." These are smart, capable young people who've been conditioned to believe they don't belong in tech.

That conditioning starts early. When a child tries to use technology and struggles, and there's no one to help them because the adults don't understand it either, they internalize that struggle as personal failure. "I can't do this. It's too hard. It's not for me."

When a child sees tech jobs and tech success stories and everyone in those stories is white or Asian, they internalize that too. "People like me don't do this. This isn't my world." When a child attends a school that doesn't teach tech skills while knowing that schools in wealthy neighborhoods do, they internalize the message that they're not worth investing in.

All of this creates a confidence gap that becomes self-fulfilling. Children who believe they can't succeed in tech don't try. Children who don't try don't develop skills. Children without skills don't pursue tech opportunities. Children who don't pursue tech opportunities don't succeed in tech. And the cycle continues.

A psychologist who works with youth told me: "I see Black teenagers who are incredibly bright, who could absolutely succeed in tech, but they won't even try because they're convinced they'll fail. That's not innate. That's learned. They learned it from a society that tells them tech isn't for people like them, from schools that don't invest in their tech education, from families that don't have the knowledge to support them. We're creating learned helplessness around technology in a generation of Black children. And that learned helplessness will limit them their entire lives."

Our children are watching us struggle with technology. They're seeing us intimidated by AI, unsure about using new tools, left behind by technological change. And they're learning from that.

If we model confidence with technology, they'll develop confidence. If we model insecurity and avoidance, they'll learn that too.

Right now, we're teaching them that technology is something to be intimidated by rather than something they can master.

The Generational Trauma of Being Left Behind

There's a psychological term that's relevant here: generational trauma. It's when trauma experienced by one generation gets passed down to the next generation and affects their mental health, behavior, and opportunities.

We usually think of this in the context of historical trauma, slavery, segregation, and discrimination. But there's also economic and technological trauma.

Our generation is experiencing the trauma of technological displacement. We're watching jobs disappear. We're seeing opportunities we don't understand and can't access. We're feeling left behind by a rapidly changing world. That's traumatic.

And our children are watching it happen.

They're watching their parents lose jobs to automation. They're watching adults in their community struggle to adapt to technological change. They're seeing the stress, the financial insecurity, the anxiety about the future.

That creates trauma for them too. The trauma of watching their parents be hurt by forces beyond their control. The trauma of insecurity and instability. The trauma of feeling like the world is changing in ways that threaten their family. And it creates expectations. If they watched their parents get left behind by technological change, they expect the same will happen to them. They internalize the belief that their family and community just don't succeed with technology.

That's generational trauma. And it becomes self-fulfilling unless we break the cycle. A therapist working with Black families told me: "I'm seeing children with anxiety about the future. Ten and twelve-year-olds worried about whether they'll be able to get jobs, whether AI will take all the opportunities, whether they'll be okay. That's not normal childhood anxiety. That's existential anxiety about economic survival, and they're getting it from watching their parents struggle. We're passing our technological trauma to our children."

But here's what's crucial: **generational trauma can be healed. And cycles can be broken.**

If our generation takes action, if we learn about AI, if we position ourselves and our families for the AI economy, and if we model confidence and engagement with technology rather than fear and avoidance, we can break this cycle.

We can be the generation that stopped being left behind and the parents who prepared their children for the future. But only if we act.

What Our Ancestors Sacrificed

I need you to think about your ancestors for a moment.

Think about enslaved people who risked everything to learn to read when it was illegal, when the punishment could be death, because they understood that literacy was power and they wanted their children to have that power.

Think about people who walked miles to one-room schoolhouses during Jim Crow, who studied by candlelight, who went without so their children could go to school, because they understood that education was the pathway to a better future.

Think about parents during segregation who fought to integrate schools, who faced violence and hatred, who endured because they believed their children deserved equal education.

Think about grandparents who worked multiple jobs, who sacrificed their own comfort and health, so their children and grandchildren could go to college, could have opportunities they never had.

Every generation of our ancestors sacrificed so the next generation would have better opportunities.

They endured. They fought. They persisted. Even when it was dangerous. Even when it seemed impossible. Because they believed in the next generation's potential and they refused to accept that their children would be limited by the same forces that limited them.

What are we doing for our children?

Are we fighting to ensure they have AI literacy? Are we

sacrificing to give them access to technological education? Are we preparing them for the future economy? Are we breaking the cycle of technological exclusion?

Or are we letting them inherit our limitations?

Our ancestors didn't survive slavery so their descendants could be left behind by algorithms. They didn't endure Jim Crow so we could watch our children get excluded from the digital economy. They didn't fight for civil rights so we could accept technological subjugation.

We owe them more than that. We owe our children more than that.

A historian who studies Black resistance told me: "Every generation has had to fight a different form of oppression. Slavery. Segregation. Discrimination. Now it's technological exclusion and algorithmic bias. The form changes but the fight doesn't. And each generation has a responsibility to fight their era's fight so the next generation starts from a better place. What will history say about how we responded to the AI revolution? Did we fight? Or did we let our children down?"

The Legacy We're Leaving

Let's talk about legacy.

What are you going to leave your children? What will they inherit from you?

If we sit out the AI revolution, here's what they inherit:

- Economic disadvantage in an AI-powered economy
- Skills gaps that limit their career options
- Technological insecurity that limits their confidence

- Lack of wealth that limits their opportunities
- Continued exclusion from the industries creating value
- The trauma of watching another generation get left behind

If we engage with the AI revolution, here's what they can inherit:

- Economic positioning in the AI economy
- Skills and knowledge that open opportunities
- Technological confidence that enables success
- Wealth that creates stability and opportunity
- Participation in value-creating industries
- The inspiration of watching a generation break the cycle

The difference is stark. And the choice is ours.

A parent I spoke with said something powerful: "I don't want my son to have the same conversation with his kids that I'm having with him. I don't want him to have to explain why his generation got left behind too. I want to be able to tell him, 'I saw the AI revolution coming and I prepared you for it. You have opportunities I didn't have because I made sure you were ready.' That's the legacy I want to leave."

That should be the legacy we all want to leave.

What They Need From Us Now

So what do our children need from us? Let me be specific.

They need us to learn. Even if we feel intimidated. Even if it's hard. Even if we're starting from behind. They need us to model lifelong learning and technological engagement.

They need us to teach them or get them taught, through free resources, mentors, programs, or our own guidance, so they have access to AI education.

They need us to encourage their curiosity about technology and support their interest instead of dismissing it.

They need us to connect them with opportunities like coding clubs, tech camps, online communities, and mentorship programs.

They need us to advocate for them by pushing for better tech education and removing barriers. And they need us to build wealth through AI so we can fund their education, support their ventures, and give them the safety net to take risks.

They need us to believe in them. Even if we don't fully understand the technology, we need to believe they can master it. We need to tell them they belong in tech spaces. We need to counter the societal messages that tech isn't for people like us.

They need us to break the cycle. They need us to be the generation that stopped accepting technological exclusion and started fighting for technological empowerment.

A teacher told me: "The kids I work with are capable of anything. But they need support. They need adults who believe in them, who invest in them, who prepare them for the future. If the adults in their lives are checked out or intimidated by technology, the kids suffer. But if the adults step up, learn, engage, and advocate, those kids will do amazing things."

The Kids Who Are Winning Are Learning Now

Let me tell you about some kids I know who are winning.

Marcus, 13: Started learning Python at age 10 with free online tutorials. By 12, he was experimenting with AI tools. By 13, he'd built a chatbot to help his grandmother with medication reminders. He's applying to specialized tech high schools and will likely get significant scholarships because he has a portfolio of projects showing his capabilities.

Zara, 15: Used AI image generators to create art that she's selling online. She's making $500-$1,000 a month, which she's saving for college. She's also teaching younger kids in her community how to use creative AI tools. She sees AI as a tool for creative expression and entrepreneurship.

Darius, 11: Obsessed with how AI works. He watches videos explaining AI concepts. He asks his father (who learned about AI specifically to support his son's interest) to explain things. He talks about wanting to work in AI research someday. He has eight years to develop that interest before college, and by then he'll be far ahead of peers who discover AI for the first time in college.

Keisha, 14: Uses AI writing tools to help with homework, but more importantly, she's learning to evaluate AI outputs critically. She can spot when AI is wrong or biased. She understands AI as a tool to enhance her own thinking, not replace it. That critical thinking will serve her well in any field she pursues.

These kids have something in common: adults in their lives who ensured they had access to AI education and encouraged their engagement with technology.

Marcus's parents bought him a cheap laptop and found free resources. Zara's aunt showed her AI art generators. Darius's father learned about AI alongside his son. Keisha's teacher showed her how to use AI tools responsibly.

None of these kids are from wealthy families. None had expensive private tutors or elite schools. They just had adults who understood that AI literacy matters and made sure they had access.

That's what our children need from us. Not perfection. Not expertise. Just commitment to ensuring they have access and support.

A youth development specialist told me: "The kids who are succeeding with technology aren't necessarily the ones with the most resources. They're the ones whose adults prioritized their tech education. A parent with a smartphone and internet access can give their kid access to AI learning. It's not about money. It's about understanding that it matters and making it a priority."

The Clock Is Ticking

Here's the urgency I need you to feel: **childhood doesn't wait.**

A child who is 10 years old today will be 20 in ten years. By then, AI will be ubiquitous. The opportunities for people with AI skills will be established. The gaps between those who learned early and those who didn't will be set.

If that 10-year-old spends the next ten years not learning about AI, they'll enter adulthood unprepared. And catching up will be much harder than learning now would be.

Children's brains are wired to learn. They can pick up new concepts faster than adults. They can develop fluency with tools more easily. The earlier they start, the more natural it becomes.

If we wait until they're teenagers to worry about their AI education, we've lost years when learning would have been easier and more foundational.

If we wait until they're adults, we've lost the entire developmental period when technological literacy should have been built.

There's a window. And it's closing.

Every year we delay is a year our children fall further behind their peers who are learning now. Every year is harder to make up later.

A neuroscientist told me: "Children's brains are incredibly plastic. They can learn new skills and develop new cognitive frameworks easily. But that plasticity decreases with age. If you want your child to develop fluency with AI, to see it as a natural tool they're comfortable with, you need to start now, while their brain is most receptive. Waiting doesn't help. It just makes everything harder."

This Is Our Test

Every generation faces tests. Moments that determine whether they protect the next generation or fail them. Whether they rise to meet challenges or shrink from them. Whether they break cycles or perpetuate them.

This is our test.

Our ancestors faced their tests. Slavery. Segregation. Jim Crow. Civil rights struggles. They met those tests with courage, sacrifice, and determination. They didn't all succeed perfectly, but they fought. They didn't give up. They made sure the next generation had more than they had.

Now it's our turn. The test is different, it's about technology and economic opportunity rather than explicit legal discrimination, but it's still a test.

Will we prepare our children for the AI-powered future? Or will we let them be left behind?

Will we break the cycle of technological exclusion? Or will we pass it on?

Will we be the generation that stepped up? Or the generation that failed to act?

Our children are watching us. They're seeing how we respond to this moment. And they're learning from what they see.

If they see us learning, engaging, and fighting for their future, they'll learn to do the same. If they see us intimidated, passive, and accepting exclusion, they'll learn that too.

What are we teaching them right now?

A community elder told me: "Every generation has to decide what they're going to be. Are they going to be the generation that accepted defeat? Or the generation that fought back? Are they going to be remembered for what they enabled for the next generation, or for what they failed to do? This is that decision point for your generation. Ten years from now, when your kids are adults, what will you have given them? Skills or excuses? Opportunity or limitation? A fighting chance or inherited disadvantage?"

The Hope and the Choice

I don't want to end this chapter on fear. Yes, the stakes are high. Yes, there's urgency. But there's also hope.

Our children are capable of amazing things. They're smart, creative, resilient, and talented. Given the opportunity, they can succeed with AI just as well as any other kids in the world.

The question isn't whether they can do it. The question is whether we'll give them the chance.

And that's a choice we make every day.

Every day we can choose to learn something about AI so we can teach them or support them.

Every day we can choose to connect them to resources, opportunities, and knowledge.

Every day we can choose to encourage rather than discourage their interest in technology.

Every day we can choose to model confidence rather than fear.

Every day we can choose to fight for their future rather than accept their exclusion.

Small choices, repeated daily, create different outcomes.

A child whose parent spends 30 minutes a day exploring AI tools with them is getting 182 hours of learning per year. After five years, that's over 900 hours of experience with AI.

That's enough to build real fluency and confidence.

A child whose parent stays informed about AI opportunities in their community and makes sure to connect them is being positioned for success.

A child whose parent tells them "you can do this, you belong here, this technology is for you too" is developing confidence that will carry them through challenges.

We don't have to be perfect. We don't have to be experts. We just have to care enough to try.

That's the hope. That it's not too late. That we can still act. That our choices matter. That our children's futures aren't predetermined, but depend on what we do now.

The legacy we leave them isn't set yet. We're still writing it.

Because part of preparing our children for the future is teaching them about our past. Teaching them that they come from people who built and created despite every obstacle. Teaching them that technology and innovation aren't foreign to us, they're part of who we are.

But before we go there, I need you to make a commitment.

Commit to doing one thing this week for the young people in your life regarding AI. Learn something about AI so you can explain it to them. Find one free resource and share it with them. Have one conversation about AI and why it matters. Connect them with one opportunity. Just one thing.

Then next week, do another thing. And the week after that, another.

Small actions, repeated consistently, will prepare our children for the future.

They're counting on us. They might not know it yet. They might not be asking for it. But they need us to step up.

We can't let them down.

Our ancestors didn't let us down. They fought for us even when it was hard, even when it was dangerous, even when success wasn't guaranteed.

Now it's our turn to fight for the next generation.

Let's not be the generation that failed them.

Let's be the generation that prepared them. That empowered them. That gave them the tools and knowledge they need to succeed in an AI-powered world.

Let's be the generation that broke the cycle.

Our children are watching.

Let's show them what fighting for the future looks like.

www.BlaqGPT.com

www.ingramcontent.com/pod-product-compliance
Lightning Source LLC
LaVergne TN
LVHW020708110826
845149LV00012B/2168

* 9 7 9 8 9 9 5 5 8 9 4 8 8 *